tempted

150 very wicked desserts

Published in 2006 by Murdoch Books Pty Limited
www.murdochbooks.com.au

Murdoch Books Australia
Pier 8/9, 23 Hickson Road, Millers Point
NSW 2000
Phone: +61 (0)2 8220 2000 Fax: +61 (0)2 8220 2558

Chief Executive: Juliet Rogers
Publishing Director: Kay Scarlett

Design Manager: Vivien Valk
Project Manager and Editor: Janine Flew
Food Editor: Joanne Glynn
Design Concept: Marylouise Brammer
Art Direction and Designer: Sarah Odgers
Photographer: Brett Stevens
Stylist: Vanessa Austin
Food preparation: Grace Campbell, Joanne Kelly, Wendy
Quisumbing
Recipes: Michelle Earl, Joanne Glynn, Wendy Quisumbing
and the Murdoch Books Test Kitchen
General and chapter introductions: Margaret Malone
Production: Adele Troeger

National Library of Australia
Cataloguing-in-Publication Data
Tempted : 150 very wicked desserts. Includes index.
ISBN 978 1 74045 817 7. ISBN 1 74045 817 6.
1. Desserts. I. Title. (Series : Retro series) 641.86

Printed by Midas Printing (Asia) Ltd in 2006.
PRINTED IN CHINA

Murdoch Books UK Limited
Erico House, 6th Floor North, 93–99 Upper Richmond Road
Putney, London SW15 2TG
Phone: +44 (0) 20 8785 5995 Fax: +44 (0) 20 8785 5985

IMPORTANT: Those who might be at risk from the effects
of salmonella poisoning (the elderly, pregnant women,
young children and those suffering from immune deficiency
diseases) should consult their doctor with any concerns
about eating raw eggs.

The publisher and stylist would like to thank the following
companies for generously lending furniture, fabric,
tableware, floor coverings, paint, clothes and wallpaper
for photography: 224 Bondi Rd; Bodum; Brunschwig
and Fils; Chee Soon and Fitzgerald; Cloth; Country Road;
Dandi; Dinosaur Designs; Domayne Design Centre;
Dulux (Designer silk range); ECC Lighting; Elevate Designs;
Hoglund Art Glass; Husk; Jarass; Jendi; Laminex; Le Forge;
Love Plates for VNR Australia; Major and Tom; Maxwell
and Williams; Mokum Textiles; Mud Australia; Newtown
Old Wares; Osborne and Little; Pazotti; Perry and Fowles;
Primo Imports; Radford Furnishings; Rosenthal—Studio
Line; South Pacific Fabrics; Spence and Lyda; Studio
Imports; The Source Products; Tomkin Australia; Tres Fabu.

CONVERSION GUIDE: You may find cooking times vary
depending on the oven you are using. For fan-forced
ovens, as a general rule, set the oven temperature to
20°C (35°F) lower than indicated in the recipe. We have
used 20 ml (4 teaspoon) tablespoon measures. If you
are using a 15 ml (3 teaspoon) tablespoon, for most
recipes the difference will not be noticeable. However,
for recipes using baking powder, gelatine, bicarbonate
of soda (baking soda), small amounts of flour and
cornflour (cornstarch), add an extra teaspoon for each
tablespoon specified.

tempted

150 very wicked desserts

Photography by Brett Stevens
Styling by Vanessa Austin

MURDOCH BOOKS

contents

the sweet life People have taken delight and pride in creating delicious and eleborate desserts for as long as there have been bowls to mix with and fires to cook over. Whether decadent and

rich or simple and quick to make, all fabulous desserts have a common theme — the enjoyment of eating them is more than matched by the pleasure taken in their making.

the sweet life

It's a secret shared by all cooks that cooking a dessert is no chore. People who don't cook marvel at a home-made chocolate cake or a pile of still-warm brownies, convinced that the skills needed to produce such wonders are far beyond them. This is a shame, because those who do cook know it's fun, it's generally easy, and what's more it's hugely rewarding. This can be true of all cooking, but it often isn't — time pressures and the necessity of producing a tasty, nutritional meal for the family night after night can mean that everyday cooking is just that — everyday. So, when the decision is taken to prepare a delicious dessert, it's not only the recipients that are very pleased with the turn of events. The cook is too.

Often, it takes only the gentlest nudge for the dessert-chef within to awaken. It might be the purchase of a bag of fresh nectarines, or simply the change of season that turns your thoughts to loved ones and what would be pleasing for their tummies. But whatever the reason, the delight in cooking dessert begins with making that decision. From there on, at every stage, it's the same; anticipation and

8

enjoyment. Turning the pages of a cookbook, choosing the recipe, doing the planning and shopping, then onto the cooking and decorating, the serving and, of course, the eating. This may sound unlikely to those unfamiliar with the delight felt upon successfully making a lemon tart from scratch or a perfect fig and raspberry cake. But what they fail to consider is that shopping for dessert wine or good-quality mascarpone cheese is not the same as buying chops, and piping chocolate icing is not the same as mashing potatoes. We enjoy it.

That is the guiding principle behind this book. Most of us don't make a dessert every day, or even every second day, so when we do, we want it to be wonderful — not just the result but the cooking, too. Thus the recipes here aren't out to shock but to satisfy. There is nothing tricksy just for the sake of it. Presentation is important, but that needn't imply fussiness. Equally, some recipes do involve a number of steps but there are none that require days and nights in the kitchen, rare and unusual ingredients or obscure pieces of equipment. What creaming and beating, mixing and baking there is falls within the bounds of healthy effort. Ingredients, too, are almost entirely familiar. It's a constant **wonder** of chemistry how flour, eggs, sugar, butter, cocoa and cream can produce time and again a new and equally irresistible creation with just a few changes in technique and some variations in supporting ingredients. With the welcome presence of fruit and nuts, or the **felicitous** addition of alcohol, the basic building blocks of desserts start to look impressive indeed.

Without further ado, then, let us turn to the recipes themselves. This collection features a little bit of everything, so it's a good book to explore. The six chapters are divided by type, and the recipes range from a **traditional** crème caramel or classic brandy-laced tiramisu to light and pretty toffee-glazed poached peaches and never-fail winners such as baked chocolate puddings with rich chocolate sauce. You can be guided in your decision-making by a particular ingredient (the last of the Cointreau in the bottle); an **occasion** (your turn to host the monthly book club meeting); the season (cherries have arrived!); or plain old **whim** (you just want to cook something sweet).

Is it too much to say there is a touch of romance in making a dessert? The creativity involved in the planning and cooking, the act of giving, the exploration of an unfamiliar or foreign recipe; these all lift us out of our everyday routine for a moment. Making Italian chocolate-filled ravioli or baked apples with Pedro Ximénez sauce — Spain's legendary sherry — does indeed conjure a little bit of Italian good living or Andalusian sunshine. Such desserts let you travel the world for a delicious brief while. This is true of a lot of good cooking, of course, but whereas with a lamb chop you're travelling economy, with a rich gateau or sumptuous soufflé, you're going Concorde. If only more of life was like this, really.

Tempted is all about enjoyment and letting your imagination lead the way — regardless of whether the chosen dish is a simple sundae or an elaborate layered frozen dessert. Once the dessert is ready, choose some nice plates, get out the good napkins, bring out the dessert forks; it's all part of the pleasure. And what's more, everyone will love it and you all the more.

chocolate heaven If these rich, dark, decadent recipes are anything to go by, chocolate heaven is a land permanently locked in winter's embrace. In this wondrously hedonistic place, the

elements conspire to keep you contentedly indoors, snuggling on the sofa and warming yourself from the inside out with a luscious helping of one of these chocolate-laden desserts.

When it comes to warding off the wintry blues, few things have the restorative powers of an indulgent slice of something heavily dependent on chocolate. Smooth and creamy, heady in its sweet richness, chocolate is the ultimate dessert-maker. Even the names of the cakes and puddings, tortes and slices in this chapter send a happy tingling through the body — wicked walnut and chocolate plum torte, rich chocolate and whisky mud cake, three chocolates tart. There is a grand, almost hedonistic tone to these recipes that brooks no resistance — chocolate filling, chocolate topping, and a bit more chocolate lovingly coating the sides. It is chocolate's wonderful versatility that makes it such a magical and pleasurable ingredient to work with in the kitchen, be it dark, milk or white, chopped and melted, blended and baked, gloopily liquid or in chunky choc bits. And when the remaining assembled ingredients include cream, sugar, eggs, nuts, liqueurs and cognacs, cinnamon and the odd marshmallow, you know that these are recipes prepared to jump in at the deep end. It is no wonder that few chefs complain about being trapped in the kitchen when it comes to chocolate creations. So, for those of us without a crackling wood fire, cosy, wood-panelled room or faithful dog resting by our feet, defending ourselves against the rigors of winter (or any season, really) need not send us packing for sunnier shores. Instead, just turn these pages and discover how many decadent, chocolate-coated ways there are to have a little bit of heaven deliciously close by.

chocolate pots with hazelnut toffee

250 g (9 oz/1^2/$_3$ cups) good-
quality dark chocolate
580 ml (20^1/$_4$ fl oz/2^1/$_3$ cups)
pouring (whipping) cream
6 large egg yolks
80 g (2^3/$_4$ oz/^{1}/$_3$ cup) caster
(superfine) sugar
1 tablespoon freshly brewed
espresso coffee

2 tablespoons Frangelico or
other hazelnut liqueur

95 g (3^1/$_4$ oz/^{2}/$_3$ cup) whole
hazelnuts, toasted and
skinned (see Note, page 41)
230 g (8 oz/1 cup) caster
(superfine) sugar

Preheat the oven to 150°C (300°F/ Gas 2). Finely chop the chocolate and put it in a heatproof bowl.

Gently heat the cream in a small saucepan over medium heat. Bring it just to a simmer (don't allow it to boil), then quickly remove it from the heat and pour it over the chocolate. Stir constantly until the chocolate has completely melted — this will take about 5 minutes. The mixture should be smooth and have an even colour.

Whisk the egg yolks with the sugar just to combine, then gradually stir in the chocolate mixture, then the coffee and liqueur. Strain the mixture through a fine sieve. Allow to settle and cool slightly, then skim off any foam on the surface.

Divide the mixture among eight 125 ml (4 fl oz/$^1/_2$ cup) ramekins, filling to just below the top. If there are any air bubbles on the surface, gently prick them with a fine skewer or tap the ramekin lightly on the bench.

Cover each ramekin tightly with foil. Put the ramekins into a large baking dish, ensuring they are evenly spaced and not too close to the edge of the dish, then pour in enough hot water to reach about halfway up the sides of the ramekins. Cook for 1 hour, then check them by gently shaking a ramekin — the mixture should be set around the edges but still wobble a little in the middle.

Take the ramekins out of the pan, remove the foil and allow them to cool completely before covering and refrigerating for at least 3 hours, or until well chilled. Serve the chocolate pots accompanied by the hazelnut toffee.

For the toffee, spread the hazelnuts on a lightly buttered baking tray. Put the sugar and 250 ml (9 fl oz/1 cup) water in a small pan over high heat and stir until the sugar has dissolved. Bring to the boil, then reduce the heat and simmer for 8 minutes, or until the toffee has turned a deep amber, swirling the pan occasionally so that it cooks evenly, and watching carefully so that it doesn't become too dark. Take off the heat immediately and pour the toffee over the hazelnuts on the tray. Put aside and allow to set. When cool, break into uneven pieces.

Serves 8

chocolate roulade with black cherry kirsch cream

3 eggs
115 g (4 oz/$\frac{1}{2}$ cup) caster
    (superfine) sugar
2 teaspoons instant coffee
    granules
60 g (2$\frac{1}{4}$ oz/$\frac{1}{2}$ cup) self-raising
    flour
40 g (1$\frac{1}{2}$ oz/$\frac{1}{3}$ cup)
    unsweetened cocoa powder
30 g (1 oz/$\frac{1}{4}$ cup) grated dark
    chocolate

1 tablespoon caster (superfine)
    sugar, extra

185 ml (6 fl oz/$\frac{3}{4}$ cup)
    thickened (whipping) cream
1 tablespoon icing
    (confectioners') sugar
425 g (15 oz) tin pitted black
    cherries, drained and halved
160 g (5$\frac{1}{2}$ oz/$\frac{1}{2}$ cup) cherry jam
2 tablespoons kirsch

unsweetened cocoa powder,
    to dust (optional)
icing (confectioners') sugar,
    to dust (optional)

Preheat the oven to 180ºC (350ºF/Gas 4). Grease a 25 x 30 cm (10 x 12 inch) Swiss roll (jelly roll) tin and line with baking paper. Using electric beaters, beat the eggs in a medium bowl for 2 minutes, until pale and thick. Gradually add the sugar in a slow steady stream, then continue to beat for a further 3 minutes until the mixture is thick and creamy.

Dissolve the coffee in 1 tablespoon boiling water. Sift together the flour and cocoa powder. Using a large metal spoon, fold the sifted flour and cocoa, the chocolate and dissolved coffee into the egg mixture. Mix quickly and lightly. Spread evenly into the prepared tray and smooth the surface. Bake for 12 minutes or until springy to the touch.

Put a sheet of baking paper on a clean tea towel (dish towel). Sprinkle the baking paper with the extra caster sugar. Turn the cake out onto the paper and carefully remove the baking paper used for lining the tin. Leave for 2 minutes, then roll up the cake and baking paper from one short end and set aside for 5 minutes, or until cool.

Meanwhile, beat the cream and icing sugar until thick, then fold through the cherries. Combine the jam and kirsch in a small bowl. Carefully unroll the cake. Trim the long edges with a sharp knife to neaten. Evenly spread with the jam and kirsch mixture. Spread the cream and cherries over the cake, leaving a 5 cm (2 inch) edge on the short side furthest from you. Roll up with the aid of the baking paper, enclosing the cream and cherries.

Sprinkle liberally with the cocoa powder and icing sugar. With the seam underneath, carefully lift the roulade onto a plate. Serve immediately or cover with plastic wrap and refrigerate for up to 1 hour. Cut into thick slices to serve.

Serves 8–10

chocolate roulade with black cherry
kirsch cream

creamy chocolate mousse

125 g (4¹/2 oz/heaped ³/4 cup)
   chopped dark chocolate
4 eggs, separated
185 ml (6 fl oz/ ³/4 cup)
   thickened (whipping) cream

extra whipped cream, to serve
unsweetened cocoa powder,
   to serve

Melt the chocolate in a heatproof bowl set over a saucepan of simmering water, making sure the base of the bowl does not touch the water. Stir until smooth, then remove from the heat to cool slightly. Lightly beat the egg yolks and stir them into the chocolate. Lightly whip the cream and gently fold it into the chocolate mixture until it is velvety.

Beat the egg whites to soft peaks. Using a metal spoon, fold one spoonful of the egg white into the mousse to lighten it, then gently fold in the remainder — the secret is to use a light, quick touch.

You only need small quantities of the mousse — spoon it into six small wine glasses or six 185 ml (6 fl oz/³/4 cup) ramekins. Cover with plastic wrap and refrigerate until set, about 4 hours, or overnight. When ready to serve, add some whipped cream and a dusting of cocoa powder.

Serves 6

chocolate rum fondue

250 g (9 oz/1^2/$_3$ cups) chopped
    dark chocolate
125 ml (4 fl oz/^{1}/$_2$ cup) pouring
    (whipping) cream
1–2 tablespoons rum

1 mandarin, tangerine or small
    orange, peeled, divided into
    segments

12 cherries with stalks
2 fresh figs, quartered
    lengthways
250 g (9 oz/1^2/$_3$ cups)
    strawberries, hulled
250 g (9 oz/2^3/$_4$ cups) white
    marshmallows

Melt the chocolate and cream in a medium heatproof bowl over a saucepan of simmering water, making sure the base of the bowl doesn't touch the water. Stir until smooth, remove from the heat and stir in the rum to taste. Pour while still warm into the fondue pot.

Arrange the fruit and marshmallows on a serving platter and serve to dip into the chocolate fondue.

Note: Use a selection of whatever fruit is in season, and if they need to be cut, choose those that don't have a moist surface.

Serves 6

chocolate swirl pavlova with dipped strawberries

60 g (2¼ oz/heaped ¾ cup) chopped dark chocolate

300 g (10½ oz) small to medium strawberries

4 egg whites

pinch cream of tartar

250 g (9 oz/heaped 1 cup) caster (superfine) sugar

250 ml (9 fl oz/1 cup) thickened (whipping) cream

1 tablespoon strawberry or raspberry liqueur

1 tablespoon icing (confectioners') sugar

3 tablespoons strawberry jam

1 tablespoon strawberry or raspberry liqueur, extra

Melt the chocolate in a small bowl over a small saucepan of simmering water, making sure that the base of the bowl does not touch the water. Dip 8 of the strawberries partially into the chocolate then put them on a sheet of baking paper and leave to set. Reserve the remaining chocolate. Hull the remaining strawberries, then cut some in half lengthways, leaving the rest whole. Refrigerate until needed.

Preheat the oven to 150°C (300°F/Gas 2). Grease a baking tray or pizza tray and line with baking paper. Using electric beaters, whisk the egg whites until firm peaks form. Add the cream of tartar, then the sugar in a

slow steady stream, beating continuously, and then continue to beat for about 5 minutes until the meringue is glossy and very thick.

Spoon one-third of the meringue onto the prepared tray and spread it into a rough 23 cm (9 inch) round. With a spoon, drizzle over one-third of the reserved melted chocolate, making swirls of chocolate in a marbled effect. Top with more meringue and chocolate drizzle, then repeat once more. Use a metal spatula to flatten slightly and smooth the surface.

Bake for about 50 minutes, or until the edges and top are dry. Turn the oven off, leave the door slightly ajar and allow the meringue to cool fully.

Beat the cream, liqueur and icing sugar until thick. To serve, turn out onto a wire rack, peel off the baking paper and invert the pavlova onto a serving platter. Spread with the whipped cream. Arrange the whole and halved strawberries over the cream, interspersing them with the chocolate-coated strawberries.

Warm the strawberry jam, then pass it through a sieve and stir in the liqueur. Use a pastry brush to coat the strawberries in a random fashion, until they look glossy. Serve at once, cut into thick wedges.

Serves 8–10

25

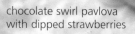

chocolate swirl pavlova
with dipped strawberries

double chocolate brownies

80 g (2³/4 oz) butter
40 g (1¹/2 oz/¹/3 cup)
   unsweetened cocoa powder
145 g (5¹/4 oz/²/3 cup) caster
   (superfine) sugar
2 eggs, lightly beaten

60 g (2¹/4 oz/¹/2 cup) plain
   (all-purpose) flour
¹/2 teaspoon baking powder
100 g (3¹/2 oz/¹/2 cup) chocolate
   chips

Preheat the oven to 180°C (350°F/Gas 4). Grease a 20 cm (8 inch) square cake tin and line with baking paper.

Melt the butter in a medium saucepan, then remove from the heat and stir in the cocoa and sugar, followed by the eggs. Sift the flour, baking powder and a pinch of salt into the saucepan, then mix it in. Make sure you don't have any pockets of flour. Stir in the chocolate chips.

Pour the mixture into the prepared tin and bake it for 30 minutes. The brownies are cooked when you can poke a skewer or knife into the middle and it comes out clean or with just a few dryish crumbs attached. (Remember that the chocolate chips may have melted and if your skewer hits one of those, it might look as if the mixture is still wet; if unsure, test in another spot.) Leave the brownies to cool in the tin, then turn out and cut into squares.

Makes 12

chocolate croissant pudding

4 croissants, torn into pieces
125 g (4^1/$_2$ oz/heaped ^{2}/$_3$ cup)
    chopped dark chocolate
4 eggs
60 g (2^1/$_4$ oz/^{1}/$_4$ cup) caster
    (superfine) sugar
250 ml (9 fl oz/1 cup) milk
250 ml (9 fl oz/1 cup) pouring
    (whipping) cream

3 teaspoons orange liqueur
3 teaspoons grated orange zest
4 tablespoons orange juice
2 tablespoons roughly chopped
    hazelnuts
thick (double/heavy) cream,
    to serve

Preheat the oven to 180°C (350°F/Gas 4). Grease a 20 cm (8 inch) round deep-sided cake tin and line the base with baking paper. Put the croissant pieces and 100 g (3^1/$_2$ oz/^{2}/$_3$ cup) of the chopped chocolate into the tin. Beat the eggs and sugar together until pale and creamy. Heat the milk, cream, liqueur and remaining chocolate in a saucepan until almost boiling. Stir to melt the chocolate, then remove the pan from the heat. Gradually add this mixture to the egg mixture, stirring constantly. Stir in the orange zest and juice. Pour the mixture over the croissants, a little at a time, allowing the liquid to be fully absorbed before adding more. Sprinkle the hazelnuts over the top and bake for 50 minutes, or until a skewer inserted into the centre comes out clean. Cool for 10 minutes. Turn out and invert onto a serving plate. Slice and serve warm with cream.

Serves 6–8

dark chocolate puddings with rich coffee liqueur mocha sauce

125 g (4¹/2 oz/ ¹/2 cup) butter,
  softened
115 g (4 oz/ ¹/2 cup) caster
  (superfine) sugar
1 teaspoon natural vanilla
  extract
2 eggs
125 g (4¹/2 oz/1 cup) plain
  (all-purpose) flour
60 g (2¹/4 oz/ ¹/2 cup)
  unsweetened cocoa powder
2 teaspoons baking powder
100 ml (3¹/2 fl oz) milk
60 g (2¹/4 oz/ heaped ¹/3 cup)
  finely chopped dark
  chocolate

coffee liqueur mocha sauce
30 g (1 oz) butter
80 g (2³/4 oz/ ¹/2 cup) chopped
  dark chocolate
170 ml (5¹/2 fl oz/ ²/3 cup)
  pouring (whipping) cream
1 teaspoon instant coffee
  granules
2 tablespoons coffee-flavoured
  liqueur (such as crème de
  cacao or Kahlùa)

35 g (1¹/4 oz/ ¹/4 cup) roasted
  hazelnuts, skinned and
  chopped (see Note, page 41)
pouring (whipping) cream,
  to serve (optional)
fresh berries, to serve (optional)

Preheat the oven to 180°C (350°F/Gas 4). Grease six 250 ml (9 fl oz/1 cup) metal moulds and put them on a baking tray. In a medium bowl, beat the butter, sugar and vanilla with electric beaters for 2 minutes until thick and creamy. Add the eggs one at a time, beating well after each addition. Fold in the combined sifted flour, cocoa and baking powder with a metal spoon, adding the milk alternately with the flour mixture. Stir in the chocolate. Spoon the mixture into the prepared moulds and smooth the surface. Bake for about 15 minutes, or until risen and just firm to the touch. Leave for 5 minutes, then run a small flat-bladed knife between the puddings and the moulds and turn them out onto a wire rack.

Meanwhile, for the sauce, combine the butter, chocolate, cream and coffee granules in a small saucepan over low heat. Stir until the chocolate is melted and the mixture is smooth. Remove from the heat and stir in the liqueur. Keep warm.

To serve, put the hot puddings on serving plates, pour over some of the sauce, scatter over a few chopped hazelnuts and serve with cream and berries, if liked.

Note: The puddings and sauce can be reheated in a microwave oven just before serving.

Serves 6

dark chocolate puddings with rich
coffee liqueur mocha sauce

Chocolate and nuts seem made for each other; adding brandy and mascarpone simply serves to turn delicious into irresistible.

chocolate and almond torte

150 g (5 1/2 oz/1 3/4 cups) flaked almonds (or 1 cup whole almonds)
1 slice pandoro (see Note) or 1 small brioche (about 40 g/1 1/2 oz)
300 g (10 1/2 oz/2 cups) chopped dark chocolate
2 tablespoons brandy
150 g (5 1/2 oz/scant 2/3 cup) unsalted butter, softened

150 g (5 1/2 oz/ 2/3 cup) caster (superfine) sugar
4 eggs
1 teaspoon natural vanilla extract (optional)
200 g (7 oz) mascarpone cheese
unsweetened cocoa powder, to dust
crème fraîche, to serve

Preheat the oven to 170°C (325°F/Gas 4). Put the almonds on a baking tray and toast in the oven for 8–10 minutes until golden brown. Allow to cool, then put the almonds and pandoro in a food processor and process until the mixture resembles breadcrumbs.

Lightly grease a 23 cm (9 inch) round springform cake tin. Tip some of the nut mixture into the tin and shake it around so that it forms a coating on the bottom and sides of the tin. Put the remaining nut mixture aside.

Gently melt the chocolate and brandy in a heatproof bowl set over a saucepan of simmering water, making sure the base of the bowl doesn't touch the water. Stir occasionally until melted. Cool slightly.

Cream the butter and sugar in the food processor or with a wooden spoon for a few minutes until light and pale. Add the melted chocolate, eggs, vanilla and mascarpone. Add the remaining nut mixture and mix well. Pour into the tin. Bake for 50–60 minutes, or until just set. Leave in the tin for 15 minutes before unmoulding. Dust with a little cocoa when cool, and serve with crème fraîche.

Note: Pandoro is a type of light, sweet Italian yeast bread.

Serves 8–10

chocolate praline crepes

filling

50 g (1³/4 oz/¹/3 cup) chopped
   milk chocolate
50 g (1³/4 oz/¹/3 cup) chopped
   dark chocolate
50 g (1³/4 oz) almond praline,
   croccante or vienna almonds
100 g (3¹/2 oz) unsalted butter,
   softened
2 tablespoons icing
   (confectioners') sugar
1 tablespoon cognac or brandy

crepes

125 g (4¹/2 oz/1 cup) plain
   (all-purpose) flour
1 tablespoon icing
   (confectioners') sugar
pinch salt
2 eggs
300 ml (10¹/2 fl oz) milk
1 tablespoon cognac or brandy
25 g (1 oz) butter, melted

unsalted butter, for frying
2 tablespoons cognac or brandy,
   to serve
thick (double/heavy) cream,
   to serve

For the filling, melt both chocolates together in a small heatproof bowl set over a saucepan of simmering water, making sure the base of the bowl doesn't touch the water, and stirring frequently. Cool. In a small food processor, or using a sharp knife, chop the almond praline. Don't pulverize it, but leave it with some texture. Stir it through the chocolate mixture.

Beat the butter and icing sugar with electric beaters until light and fluffy. Stir in the cognac and chocolate mixture. Cover and refrigerate until solid.

For the crepes, sift the flour, icing sugar and a pinch of salt into a bowl. Lightly beat the eggs, milk, cognac and butter in a jug then pour into the flour mixture. Beat until you have a smooth, light batter. Cover and set aside to rest for about 30 minutes.

Melt a little butter in a 20 cm (8 inch) crepe pan over medium–low heat. Pour in a small ladleful of batter, 2–3 tablespoons, and quickly swirl the pan so that the batter spreads evenly over the bottom. You want the crepes as thin as possible. Cook until bubbles start to appear in the centre and the edges become crisp. Flip the crepe over and brown the other side. Transfer to a tray and repeat with the rest of the batter. You will need 8 crepes, and there is enough mixture for a trial run.

Preheat a grill (broiler) to high. Put some chocolate filling down the centre of each crepe and roll it up. Arrange the filled crepes in a shallow heatproof dish. Put under the grill for 45–50 seconds, or until the chocolate filling melts, then remove. Immediately sprinkle the cognac over the top and carefully put a flame to it. The cognac will ignite and burn off the alcohol. Serve at once, with thick cream.

Serves 8

chocolate praline crepes

chocolate hazelnut cake

200 g (7 oz/1$^1/_2$ cups) roasted
skinned hazelnuts (see Note)
200 g (7 oz/1$^1/_3$ cups)
chopped dark chocolate
2 teaspoons instant coffee
granules
100 g (3$^1/_2$ oz/heaped $^3/_4$ cup)
cornflour (cornstarch)
200 g (7 oz) unsalted butter,
softened

185 g (6$^1/_2$ oz/1 cup) raw or
golden caster (superfine)
sugar
4 eggs, separated
2 teaspoons hazelnut liqueur
or coffee liqueur
icing (confectioners') sugar,
to serve
chocolate flakes, to serve
(optional)
crème fraîche or vanilla ice
cream, to serve

Preheat the oven to 170°C (325°F/Gas 3). Grease a 20 cm (8 inch) round springform cake tin.

Put the hazelnuts and chocolate in a small processor fitted with the metal blade and process in 5-second bursts until finely chopped. Add the coffee granules and cornflour and process briefly to combine. Transfer to a small bowl and set aside.

Change the blade on the processor to the plastic blade. Add the butter and sugar and process in 3-second bursts until pale. Add one-quarter of the chocolate mixture, process in short bursts to combine, then add 1 egg yolk and whizz in short bursts to mix through. Continue in this way until all the chocolate mixture and egg yolks have been added. Add the liqueur and whizz in short bursts to combine. Transfer to a bowl.

Whisk the egg whites until soft peaks form. Using a metal spoon, fold a large scoop of egg white into the chocolate mixture. Gently fold in the remaining egg white. Spoon into the prepared tin, level the surface and bake for 30 minutes. Cover loosely with foil and bake for 30–35 minutes more, or until a skewer inserted in the centre of the cake comes out clean. The surface of the cake will probably crack.

Serve the cake warm or at room temperature. Dust the surface with icing sugar and sprinkle with chocolate flakes, if using. Cut the cake into slices; the texture will be quite moist. Serve with a scoop of crème fraîche or softened vanilla ice cream.

Note: To roast and skin hazelnuts, spread in a single layer in a roasting dish and toast in a moderate oven for 10 minutes or so, stirring occasionally, until fragrant and golden. Tip the hot nuts into a clean tea towel (dish towel), gather up the corners and rub to remove most of the skins. Not all of the skins will come off; don't worry about those that don't.

Serves 6–8

wicked walnut and chocolate plum torte

200 g (7 oz/2 cups) walnuts
200 g (7 oz/1 1/3 cups) chilled,
    chopped dark chocolate
2 teaspoons instant coffee
    granules
100 g (3 1/2 oz/heaped 3/4 cup)
    cornflour (cornstarch)
200 g (7 oz) butter, softened,
    plus 1 tablespoon extra
185 g (6 1/2 oz/1 cup) raw caster
    (superfine) sugar

4 eggs, separated
2 teaspoons coffee liqueur
450 g (1 lb) small firm plums
    (angelina or sugar plums are
    ideal), or 800 g (1 lb 12 oz)
    medium to large plums,
    halved, stoned
2 tablespoons dark brown sugar
vanilla ice cream or whipped
    cream, to serve

42

Preheat the oven to 170°C (325°F/Gas 3). Grease a 25 cm (10 inch) round springform cake tin and line the base with baking paper.

Grind the walnuts and chocolate together in a food processor until finely processed. Add the coffee granules and cornflour and process briefly to combine.

In a large bowl, cream the butter and sugar with electric beaters until pale. Add the egg yolks, one at a time, alternately with some of the walnut mixture, beating well after each addition. Stir in the liqueur.

Whisk the egg whites until soft peaks form. Fold a large spoonful into the walnut mixture, then gently fold the rest of the egg white through. Spoon into the prepared tin and level the surface. Bake for 30 minutes.

Remove the cake from the oven and arrange the plums on top of the cake, cut side up. Scatter the brown sugar over them and dot the extra 1 tablespoon butter over the sugar. Return the cake to the oven and bake for about 40 minutes longer, or until a skewer inserted in the centre comes out clean.

Remove the torte from the oven and cool for 1 minute, then carefully run a knife around the edge to prevent any toffee sticking to the tin. Cool in the tin for 15 minutes before turning out onto a wire rack. Serve warm in slices, accompanied by softened vanilla ice cream or whipped cream.

Serves 8–10

wicked walnut and chocolate
plum torte

Sweetened dried cranberries (sometimes marketed as craisins) add a slight chewiness to this nut-flavoured meringue gateau.

white chocolate, almond and cranberry torte

8 egg whites
200 g (7 oz) caster (superfine)
    sugar
250 g (9 oz/1²/3 cups) chopped
    good-quality white chocolate
200 g (7 oz/1¹/4 cups) whole
    blanched almonds, toasted
    then chopped

200 g (7 oz/1¹/2 cups) sweetened
    dried cranberries
40 g (1¹/2 oz/¹/3 cup) self-raising
    flour

Preheat the oven to 180°C (350°F/Gas 4). Grease a 24 cm (9¹/2 inch) round springform cake tin and line the base with baking paper. Dust the inside of the tin with a little flour, shaking out any excess.

Using electric beaters, whisk the egg whites in a clean, dry bowl until stiff peaks form. Gradually add the sugar, whisking well after each addition. Whisk until the mixture is stiff and glossy and all the sugar has dissolved.

Put the chocolate, almonds and cranberries into a bowl, add the flour and toss to combine. Gently fold the chocolate mixture into the egg whites. Spread the mixture into the prepared tin and gently tap the base on a work surface.

Bake for 1 hour, covering the cake with foil halfway through cooking if it begins to brown too quickly. Turn off the oven and leave the cake to cool completely in the oven. Run a knife around the edge of the tin to loosen the torte, then remove it from the tin.

The torte will keep, stored in an airtight container in a cool place, for up to 1 week. It is not suitable to freeze.

Serves 8–10

chocolate malakoff

100 ml (3$^{1}/_2$ fl oz/$^{1}/_3$ cup) coffee liqueur

250 g (9 oz) savoiardi (sponge finger biscuits), preferably small ones

60 g (2$^{1}/_4$ oz/heaped $^{1}/_3$ cup) chopped dark chocolate

125 g (4$^{1}/_2$ oz/$^{1}/_2$ cup) unsalted butter, softened

125 g (6$^{1}/_2$ oz/$^{2}/_3$ cup) raw caster (superfine) sugar

$^{1}/_2$ teaspoon natural vanilla extract

125 g (4$^{1}/_2$ oz/1$^{1}/_4$ cups) ground almonds

150 ml (5 fl oz) thickened (whipping) cream, whipped

150 g (5$^{1}/_2$ oz/1$^{1}/_4$ cups) fresh or thawed frozen raspberries, plus extra fresh raspberries, to serve (optional)

unsweetened cocoa powder, to dust

icing (confectioners') sugar, to dust

Line a 1.5 litre (52 fl oz/6 cup) pudding basin with plastic wrap, allowing enough overhang to use as handles when unmoulding. Mix half the liqueur with 1 tablespoon water in a small plate. Dip the smooth sides of the savoiardi briefly into the liquid and use them to neatly line the bottom and sides of the basin, smooth sides inwards. Stand them upright around the sides, and trim them to fit snugly.

Melt the chocolate in a small heatproof bowl set over a saucepan of gently simmering water, making sure that the base of the bowl does not touch the water, and stirring frequently. Remove the bowl from the heat and stir in the remaining coffee liqueur, including any liquid left over from dipping the biscuits.

Cream the butter and sugar with electric beaters until pale and fluffy. Fold through the melted chocolate. Add the vanilla and almonds and fold in lightly but thoroughly. Fold in the whipped cream.

Spoon one-quarter of the mixture into the basin. Cover with one-third of the raspberries, then repeat the layering twice more. Finish with the remaining one-quarter of the mixture smoothed over the top. If you have any savoiardi left, they can go on top if you like, but this isn't essential. Cover and refrigerate overnight to set.

Use the plastic wrap to lever the pudding out of the bowl (you can also run a knife around the inside of the bowl to help loosen it), then invert it onto a serving plate. Remove the plastic wrap. Dust the top with cocoa, letting some of it drift down the sides. Lightly dust icing sugar on top of the cocoa. Cut into slices and serve with extra raspberries, if desired.

Serves 6–8

chocolate malakoff

white chocolate torte

3 eggs, at room temperature
80 g (2³/4 oz/¹/3 cup) caster
    (superfine) sugar
80 g (2³/4 oz/¹/2 cup) chopped
    white chocolate, melted
60 g (2¹/4 oz/¹/2 cup) plain
    (all-purpose) flour, sifted

topping
150 ml (5 fl oz) thickened
    (whipping) cream
250 g (9 oz/1²/3 cups) chopped
    white chocolate
125 g (4¹/2 oz/heaped ¹/2 cup)
    mascarpone cheese
white chocolate curls, to serve

Preheat the oven to 180°C (350°F/Gas 4). Grease a 21 cm (8 inch) round springform cake tin. Beat the eggs and sugar with an electric beater until thick and pale. Fold in the melted chocolate and sifted flour. Pour into the prepared tin and bake for 20 minutes, or until a skewer inserted into the centre of the cake comes out clean. Leave in the tin to cool.

For the topping, put the cream and white chocolate in a saucepan. Stir constantly over low heat for 5–6 minutes, or until the chocolate has melted and the mixture is smooth. Remove from heat and set aside to cool slightly. Stir the mascarpone into the chocolate mixture. Remove the cake from the tin and use a spatula to spread the topping over the top and sides. Refrigerate overnight, or until the topping is firm. Serve topped with the chocolate curls.

Serves 6–8

white chocolate and raspberry ripple rice pudding

120 g (4¹/4 oz/1 cup) fresh
   raspberries
2 tablespoons icing
   (confectioners') sugar
2 tablespoons raspberry liqueur,
   such as Framboise
30 g (1 oz) unsalted butter
125 g (4¹/2 oz/scant ²/3 cup)
   risotto rice

1 vanilla bean, split
800 ml (28 fl oz) milk
50 g (1³/4 oz/¹/4 cup) caster
   (superfine) sugar
1 teaspoon natural vanilla
   extract
100 g (3¹/2 oz/²/3 cup) chopped
   white chocolate

Using a hand blender, purée the raspberries, icing sugar and liqueur.

Melt the butter in a large non-stick saucepan. Add the rice and vanilla bean and stir until the rice is coated in butter. In a separate saucepan, heat the milk, caster sugar and vanilla to just below boiling. Ladle a spoonful of the milk mixture into the rice and stir constantly until the liquid has been absorbed. Repeat until all the milk mixture has been added and the rice is tender. Remove the vanilla bean (it can be dried and later re-used).

Add the white chocolate and stir until melted. Set aside for 5 minutes, then spoon the rice pudding into bowls. Swirl the raspberry purée through the rice to create a ripple effect.

Serves 4

rich chocolate and whisky mud cake with sugared violets

250 g (9 oz/1 cup) butter, chopped

200 g (7 oz/1¹/₃ cups) chopped dark chocolate

375 g (13 oz/1²/₃ cups) caster (superfine) sugar

125 ml (4 fl oz/¹/₂ cup) whisky

1 tablespoon instant coffee granules

185 g (6¹/₂ oz/1¹/₂ cups) plain (all-purpose) flour

60 g (2¹/₄ oz/¹/₂ cup) self-raising flour

40 g (1¹/₂ oz/¹/₃ cup) unsweetened cocoa powder

2 eggs, lightly beaten

3 tablespoons whisky, extra

chocolate glaze

80 ml (2¹/₂ fl oz/¹/₃ cup) pouring (whipping) cream

90 g (3¹/₄ oz/scant ²/₃ cup) chopped dark chocolate

sugared violets, to decorate (optional; see Note)

silver cachous, to decorate (optional)

Preheat the oven to 160°C (315°F/Gas2–3). Grease a 20 cm (8 inch) square tin and line the base and sides with baking paper.

Put the butter, chocolate, sugar and whisky in a saucepan. Dissolve the coffee granules in 125 ml (4 fl oz/¹/₂ cup) hot water and add to the mixture. Stir over low heat until melted and smooth.

Sift the plain flour, self-raising flour and cocoa into a large bowl. Pour the butter mixture onto the flour mixture and whisk until just combined. Whisk in the eggs. Pour into the prepared tin.

Bake for about 1 hour 15 minutes, or until a skewer comes out clean when inserted in the centre of the cake. Pour the extra whisky over the hot cooked cake. Leave in the tin for 20 minutes, then turn out onto a wire rack placed over a baking tray to cool completely.

For the chocolate glaze, put the cream in a small saucepan and bring just to the boil. Remove from the heat and add the chocolate. Stir until combined and smooth. Set aside to cool and thicken a little. Spread the glaze over the cake, allowing it to drizzle over the sides. Leave to set. Decorate with the sugared violets and silver cachous.

Note: To make the sugared violets, use a small, clean artist's paintbrush to coat 16 fresh unsprayed violets with a thin layer of lightly beaten egg white. Sprinkle evenly with caster sugar. Stand the violets on a wire rack and leave to dry. When dry, store in an airtight container between layers of tissue. The violets are edible.

Serves 16–20

rich chocolate and whisky mud cake
with sugared violets

Dense, chewy brownies are delicious just as they are, or pile them high and add candles for a birthday cake with a difference.

cashew brownies

200 g (7 oz/1^1/$_3$ cups) chopped dark chocolate

175 g (6 oz) chopped unsalted butter

2 eggs

230 g (8^1/$_2$ oz/1 cup firmly packed) dark brown sugar

40 g (1^1/$_2$ oz/^{1}/$_3$ cup) unsweetened cocoa powder

125 g (4^1/$_2$ oz/1 cup) plain (all-purpose) flour

80 g (2^3/$_4$ oz/^{1}/$_2$ cup) unsalted cashews, toasted, chopped

100 g (3^1/$_2$ oz/^{2}/$_3$ cup) chopped dark chocolate, extra

icing

200 g (7 oz/1^1/$_2$ cups) chopped dark chocolate

125 g (4^1/$_2$ oz/^{1}/$_2$ cup) sour cream

30 g (1 oz/^{1}/$_4$ cup) icing (confectioners') sugar, sifted

Preheat the oven to 160°C (315°F/Gas 2–3). Grease a 23 cm (9 inch) square cake tin and line the base with baking paper.

Melt the chocolate and butter in a heatproof bowl set over a saucepan of gently simmering water, making sure the base of the bowl does not touch the water, and stirring frequently. Allow to cool.

Whisk the eggs and sugar in a large bowl for 5 minutes, or until pale and thick. Fold in the cooled chocolate mixture, then the sifted cocoa powder and flour. Fold in the cashews and extra chocolate, then pour into the tin, smoothing the top. Bake for 30–35 minutes, or until just firm to the touch. (The brownies may have a slightly soft centre when hot but will become firm when cool.) Allow to cool.

For the icing, put the chocolate in a small heatproof bowl set over a small saucepan of gently simmering water, stirring occasionally until melted. Cool slightly, then add the sour cream and icing sugar and mix well. Spread evenly over the cooled brownies. Leave for a few hours or overnight, then cut into 25 squares. The un-iced brownies will keep, stored in an airtight container, for up to 5 days, or up to 3 months in the freezer. Thaw fully before icing.

Makes 25

devil's food cake with strawberry cream

280 g (10 oz/2¼ cups) self-
    raising flour
85 g (3 oz/⅔ cup) unsweetened
    cocoa powder
340 g (11¾ oz/1½ cups) caster
    (superfine) sugar
3 eggs, lightly beaten
150 g (5½ oz) butter, softened

chocolate curls
90 g (3¼ oz/scant ⅔ cup)
    chopped milk chocolate
90 g (3¼ oz/scant ⅔ cup)
    chopped white chocolate

ganache
225 g (8 oz1½ cups) chopped
    dark chocolate
70 g (2½ oz) butter

strawberry cream
250 ml (9 fl oz/1 cup) thickened
    (whipping) cream
2 tablespoons icing
    (confectioners') sugar
300 g (10½ oz/2 cups)
    strawberries
1 teaspoon natural vanilla
    essence

4 tablespoons strawberry jam
2 tablespoons orange liqueur,
    such as Grand Marnier or
    Cointreau
icing (confectioners') sugar

Preheat the oven to 180°C (350°F/Gas 4). Grease a 24 cm (9½ inch) round cake tin and line the base with baking paper. Sift the flour and cocoa into a large bowl. Add the sugar, eggs, butter and 250 ml (9 fl oz/

1 cup) of water. Using electric beaters, beat on low speed for 1 minute. Increase the speed to high and beat for a further 4 minutes. Pour into the prepared tin. Bake for about 55 minutes, or until a skewer inserted into the centre of the cake comes out clean. Leave in the tin for 20 minutes before turning onto a wire rack to cool completely.

For the chocolate curls, melt both chocolates separately in small heatproof bowls over (not touching) saucepans of gently simmering water. Spread separately in thin layers onto a flat surface. Allow to set. Using a knife at a 45-degree angle, form long thin curls by pushing the knife through the chocolate away from you. Refrigerate the curls until needed. For the ganache, melt the chocolate and butter in a heatproof bowl over a saucepan of gently simmering water. Set aside to cool slightly. For the strawberry cream, using electric beaters, beat the cream and icing sugar together until thick. Refrigerate until needed. Set aside 8 whole strawberries; hull and chop the remainder. Just before using, fold the chopped strawberries and vanilla through the cream. Combine the jam and liqueur in a small bowl. Cut the cake in half horizontally. Place the bottom half on a serving plate and spread evenly with the jam, then the strawberry cream. Top with the other cake half. Spread the ganache smoothly over the top of the cake. Arrange the milk and white chocolate curls and the strawberries decoratively over the cake. Dust all over with icing sugar just prior to serving. To serve, cut the cake into wedges.

Serves 8–10

devil's food cake with
strawberry cream

flourless chocolate cake

150 g (5^{1}/$_{2}$ oz oz/1 cup) chopped dark chocolate

125 g (4^{1}/$_{2}$ oz/^{1}/$_{2}$ cup) unsalted butter, chopped

150 g (5^{1}/$_{2}$ oz/^{2}/$_{3}$ cup) caster (superfine) sugar

5 eggs, separated

200 g (7 oz/1^{3}/$_{4}$ cups) ground hazelnuts

^{1}/$_{2}$ teaspoon baking powder

40 g (1^{1}/$_{2}$ oz/^{1}/$_{3}$ cup) unsweetened cocoa powder

1 teaspoon ground cinnamon

icing (confectioners') sugar, to dust

vanilla cream

1 vanilla bean or 1 teaspoon natural vanilla extract

300 ml (10^{1}/$_{2}$ fl oz) thickened (whipping) cream

1 tablespoon caster (superfine) sugar

Preheat the oven to 170°C (325°F/Gas 3). Lightly grease a 20 cm (8 inch) round cake tin and line the base with baking paper.

Melt the chocolate in a heatproof bowl set over a saucepan of gently simmering water, making sure the base of the bowl does not touch the water, and stirring frequently. Set aside and allow to cool.

Using electric beaters, cream the butter and sugar in a large bowl until pale and fluffy. Add the egg yolks one at a time, beating well after each addition. Fold in the cooled, melted chocolate.

Sift the hazelnuts, baking powder, cocoa powder and cinnamon into a bowl, then fold into the chocolate mixture.

Whisk the egg whites in a clean, dry bowl until stiff peaks form. Using a large metal spoon, fold the egg whites into the chocolate mixture, working in two batches. Gently spread the mixture into the tin and bake for about 1 hour, or until a skewer inserted into the centre of the cake comes out clean. Cool the cake in the tin.

Meanwhile, make the vanilla cream. If using the vanilla bean, split it down the middle and scrape out the seeds. Beat the cream, vanilla seeds (or vanilla extract) and sugar in a small bowl using electric beaters until soft peaks form. Dust with icing sugar before serving with the vanilla cream.

This cake will keep, stored in an airtight container, for 3–4 days. It is also suitable to freeze.

Serves 6–8

white chocolate parfait with almond praline

55 g (2 oz/¼ cup) caster
    (superfine) sugar
2 teaspoons instant coffee
    granules
125 g (4½ oz/heaped ¾ cup)
    roughly chopped white
    chocolate
3 egg yolks
3 tablespoons Marsala
250 ml (9 fl oz/1 cup) thickened
    (whipping) cream

almond praline
50 g (1¾ oz/⅓ cup) whole
    blanched almonds, lightly
    toasted, coarsely chopped
80 g (2¾ oz/⅓ cup) caster
    (superfine) sugar

extra Marsala, to drizzle

Put the sugar and 4 tablespoons water in a saucepan. Stir to dissolve the sugar, then bring to the boil. Reduce the heat and simmer for 4 minutes.

Meanwhile, dissolve the coffee in 2 teaspoons hot water. Put the white chocolate in a food processor and process until finely chopped. With the motor running, pour on the hot sugar syrup, then add the egg yolks, coffee and Marsala. Process until smooth. Transfer the mixture to a bowl.

In another bowl, beat the cream until firm. Use a metal spoon to fold the cream into the white chocolate mixture. Mix gently until smooth. Divide among six small wine glasses. Place on a tray, cover and refrigerate for at least 3 hours.

For the praline, put the almonds on a lightly greased baking tray. Put the sugar and 60 ml (2 fl oz/1/4 cup) water in a small saucepan. Stir until the sugar dissolves, then increase the heat to a boil. Boil, without stirring, for 4–5 minutes, or until the sugar caramelizes. Pour over the almonds to coat. Leave to harden, then break into pieces and roughly chop. Store in an airtight container until needed.

Before serving, place the parfaits in the freezer for about 30 minutes, until very cold. To serve, decorate with some of the praline and pour a little extra Marsala onto the parfaits. Serve immediately whilst very cold.

Serves 6

white chocolate parfait with
almond praline

three chocolates tart

pastry

150 g (5^1/2 oz/1^1/4 cups) plain
  (all-purpose) flour
20 g (^{3}/4 oz) unsweetened cocoa
  powder
75 g (2^1/2 oz) unsalted butter,
  chilled, cubed
3 tablespoons raw caster
  (superfine) sugar
4 egg yolks
^{1}/4 teaspoon natural vanilla
  extract

filling

125 g (4^1/2 oz/heaped ^{3}/4 cup)
  chopped white chocolate
3 tablespoons liquid glucose
200 g (7 oz/1^1/3 cups) chopped
  dark chocolate
300 ml (10^1/2 fl oz) thickened
  (whipping) cream

ganache

30 g (1 oz/^{1}/4 cup) chopped dark
  chocolate
15 g (^{1}/2 oz) unsalted butter
1 tablespoon pouring
  (whipping) cream

For the pastry, in a food processor, process the flour, cocoa and butter until the mixture resembles fine breadcrumbs. Add the sugar and pulse to mix through, then add the egg yolks, vanilla and 1 tablespoon water. Process to form a smooth dough. Flatten to a disc, cover with plastic wrap and chill for 45 minutes.

Preheat the oven to 180°C (350°F/Gas 4). Grease a 20 cm (8 inch) loose-based tart tin. Roll the pastry out thinly between two sheets of baking paper and use to line the prepared tin, pressing it into the flutes. Cover with a sheet of baking paper, fill with pastry weights or dried beans and bake blind for 12 minutes. Remove the baking paper and weights and bake for about 5 minutes more, or until crisp and dry. Cool completely.

For the filling, put the white chocolate in a bowl set over a saucepan of simmering water, making sure that the water doesn't touch the bottom of the bowl. Heat until melted and smooth. Spoon into the tart case and spread evenly over the bottom using the back of a spoon. Cool until set.

Put the glucose and dark chocolate in a small bowl over a saucepan of simmering water. Heat, stirring often, until melted. It will be very thick and tacky. Transfer to a bowl and cool. Whip the cream to stiff peaks. Fold a heaped spoonful of cream into the chocolate mixture to loosen it. Add the rest of the cream and fold through; the mixture will become very smooth and glossy. Spoon into the tart case, leaving it in broad swirls across the surface. Refrigerate until set.

For the ganache, put the chocolate, butter and cream in a small bowl and set over a saucepan of simmering water. Stir until smooth and glossy. Remove from the heat and cool. Spoon the ganache into a piping bag fitted with a 1–2 mm (1^1/16 inch) tip (or use a sturdy plastic bag and snip off a corner) and pipe a criss-cross pattern, like an uneven grid, over the tart. Refrigerate until set before serving. Cut into slices using a hot knife.

Serves 8

chocolate mousse meringue cake

6 eggs, separated
375 g (13 oz/1²/₃ cups) caster
    (superfine) sugar
2¹/₂ tablespoons unsweetened
    cocoa powder
1 tablespoon instant coffee
    granules

200 g (7 oz) dark chocolate,
    melted
600 ml (21 fl oz) thickened
    (whipping) cream, whipped
unsweetened cocoa powder,
    extra, to dust

Preheat the oven to 150°C (300°F/Gas 2). Cut four pieces of baking paper large enough to line four baking trays. On three of the pieces of paper, mark a 22 cm (8¹/₂ inch) circle. On the remaining piece, draw straight lines, 3 cm (1¹/₄ inches) apart. Line the baking trays with the paper.

Put the egg whites in a large, clean, dry bowl, leave for a few minutes to come to room temperature, then beat until soft peaks form. Gradually add the sugar, beating well after each addition. Beat for 5–10 minutes, until thick and glossy and all the sugar has dissolved. Gently fold the sifted cocoa into the meringue.

Divide the meringue into four portions. Spread three portions over the marked circles. Put the remaining portion in a piping bag fitted with a 1 cm (¹/₂ inch) plain piping nozzle. Pipe lines about 8 cm (3¹/₄ inches) long over the marked lines. Bake for 45 minutes, or until pale and crisp. Check the meringue strips occasionally to prevent overcooking. Turn off the oven and cool in the oven with the door ajar.

Dissolve the coffee granules in 1 tablespoon water. Put the melted chocolate in a bowl, whisk in the egg yolks and the coffee mixture, and beat until smooth. Fold in the whipped cream and mix until combined. Refrigerate until the mousse is cold and thick.

To assemble, place one meringue disc on a plate and spread with one-third of the mousse. Top with another disc and spread with half the remaining mousse. Repeat with the remaining disc and mousse. Run a knife around the edge of the meringue cake to spread the mousse evenly over the edge. Cut or break the meringue strips into short pieces and pile them on top of the cake, pressing them into the mousse. Dust with extra cocoa powder and refrigerate until firm.

Serves 10–12

chocolate mousse meringue cake

A chocoholic's dream — three layers of dense chocolate cake held together and topped with a decadently rich frosting.

chocolate ganache log

cake
200 g (7 oz) unsalted butter, softened

150 g (5¹/2 oz/²/3 cup) caster (superfine) sugar

6 eggs, at room temperature, separated

125 g (4¹/2 oz/1¹/4 cups) ground almonds

150 g (5¹/2 oz/1 cup) good-quality chopped dark chocolate, melted

ganache
150 ml (5 fl oz) pouring (whipping) cream

225 g (8 oz/1¹/2 cups) chopped good-quality dark chocolate

2 teaspoons instant coffee granules

Preheat the oven to 180°C (350°F/Gas 4). Grease a 25 x 30 cm (10 x 12 inch) shallow slice tin and line the base with baking paper. Beat the butter and sugar with electric beaters until light and fluffy. Add the egg yolks, one at a time, beating well after each addition. Stir in the ground almonds and melted chocolate. Beat the egg whites in a separate bowl until stiff peaks form, then gently fold into the chocolate mixture. Spread the mixture into the prepared tin and bake for 15 minutes. Reduce the oven to 160°C (315°F/Gas 2–3) and bake for another 30–35 minutes, or until a skewer comes out clean when inserted into the centre of the cake. Turn the cake onto a wire rack to cool.

For the ganache, put the cream and chocolate in a heatproof bowl over a saucepan of barely simmering water, making sure the base of the bowl doesn't touch the water. Stir occasionally until melted and combined. Stir in the coffee until it has dissolved. Set aside to cool for 2 hours, or until thickened to a spreading consistency.

Cut the cake horizontally into three even pieces. Place one piece on a serving plate and spread with a layer of ganache. Top with another layer of cake and another layer of ganache, followed by the remaining cake. Refrigerate for 30 minutes to set slightly. Cover the top and sides of the log with the remaining ganache and refrigerate for 3 hours, or overnight.

Serves 8–10

chocolate panna cotta with figs and hazelnuts

250 ml (9 fl oz/1 cup) pouring (whipping) cream
250 ml (9 fl oz/1 cup) milk
150 g (5 1/2 oz/1 cup) chopped dark chocolate
55 g (2 oz/1/4 cup) caster (superfine) sugar
1/2 teaspoon natural vanilla extract

3 teaspoons powdered gelatine
6 fresh figs
2 tablespoons brown sugar
whipped cream or mascarpone cheese, to serve
35 g (1 1/4 oz/1/4 cup) roasted hazelnuts, skinned and chopped (see Note, page 41)

Put the cream, milk, chocolate, sugar and vanilla in a saucepan. Stir over low heat until the mixture is smooth. Bring slowly just to the boil, then remove from the heat. Set aside.

Put the gelatine in 2 tablespoons cold water and stir to dissolve. Stir into the warm chocolate mixture. Strain the mixture into a jug then pour evenly among six 125 ml (4 fl oz/1/2 cup) dariole or ceramic moulds. Put on a tray, cover with plastic wrap and refrigerate for 4–6 hours, or overnight, until set. Even after this, it will still be quite wobbly.

To un-mould, briefly dip the moulds into hot water and loosen the edges at the top by gently easing them away from the moulds with your thumb. Turn out onto serving plates. Just prior to serving, preheat a grill (broiler). Halve the figs lengthways, drizzle each with a little of the brown sugar and grill (broil) for 3–4 minutes until hot and slightly browned.

Serve the panna cottas with the grilled figs and a dollop of the cream or mascarpone. Scatter the chopped hazelnuts on top.

Serves 6

79

chocolate panna cotta with
figs and hazelnuts

Light-as-air soufflés are not as difficult to make as their reputation alleges — and they more than repay the effort.

chocolate soufflé

175 g (6 oz/1¹/4 cups) good-quality chopped dark chocolate

5 eggs, separated

60 g (2¹/4 oz/¹/4 cup) caster (superfine) sugar, plus extra for dusting

2 egg whites, extra

icing (confectioners') sugar, for dusting

Preheat the oven to 200°C (400°F/Gas 6) and put a baking tray into the oven to warm.

Wrap a double layer of baking paper around the outside of six 250 ml (9 fl oz/1 cup) ramekins to come about 3 cm (1¹/4 inches) above the rim and secure with string. This encourages the soufflé to rise well. Brush the insides of the ramekins with melted butter and sprinkle with caster (superfine) sugar, shaking to coat evenly and tipping out any excess. This layer of butter and sugar helps the soufflé to grip the sides and rise as it cooks.

Place the chopped chocolate in a large heatproof bowl set over a saucepan of simmering water, making sure the base of the bowl does not touch the water. Stir until the chocolate is melted and smooth, then remove the bowl from the saucepan. Stir in the egg yolks and caster sugar.

Beat the 7 egg whites until stiff peaks form. Gently fold one-third of the egg whites into the chocolate mixture to loosen it. Then, using a metal spoon, fold in the remaining egg whites until just combined.

Spoon the mixture into the prepared ramekins and run your thumb or a blunt knife around the inside rim of the dish and the edge of the mixture. This ridge helps the soufflé to rise evenly. Place the ramekins on the preheated baking tray and bake for 12–15 minutes, or until well risen and just set. Do not open the oven door while the soufflés are baking.

Cut the string and remove the paper collars. Serve immediately, lightly dusted with sifted icing sugar.

Serves 6

chocolate and almond refrigerator cake

250 g (9 oz/1²/₃ cup) chopped
    dark chocolate
1 tablespoon instant coffee
    granules
250 g (9 oz/1 cup) unsalted
    butter, softened
200 g (7 oz/heaped 1 cup) raw
    caster (superfine) sugar
1 tablespoon unsweetened
    cocoa powder

3 eggs, separated
50 g (1³/₄ oz/¹/₂ cup) flaked
    almonds, toasted
50 g (1³/₄ oz/¹/₄ cup) glacé
    (candied) cherries, cut in half
300 g (10¹/₂ oz) amaretti biscuits
    (see Note)
2 tablespoons cognac

Line a 22 cm (8¹/₂ inch) springform cake tin with plastic wrap.

Melt the chocolate in a heatproof bowl set over a saucepan of simmering water, making sure the base of the bowl does not touch the water, and stirring frequently. Stir in the coffee and leave to cool.

Beat the butter and sugar with electric beaters until light and fluffy, then sift in the cocoa powder and beat well. Add the egg yolks, beating well after each addition. Fold in the melted chocolate.

In a separate clean bowl, whisk the egg whites until stiff peaks form. Gently fold into the chocolate cream using a metal spoon. Add the almonds and cherries and fold through.

Put a tightly fitting single layer of amaretti on the bottom of the prepared tin, flat side down. Drizzle a little cognac over them. Spread half the chocolate cream on top then cover with another layer of amaretti. Sprinkle with cognac, cover with the rest of the chocolate cream and put a final tight layer of amaretti on top, flat side down. Knock the tin on the bench a couple of times to pack the cake down. Cover the top with plastic wrap and refrigerate overnight.

Remove the cake from the tin. It will be sufficiently set to enable you to upturn it onto one hand, peel off the plastic wrap and set it down on a serving plate, right way up. Cut into wedges to serve.

Note: For the most attractive presentation, use the standard-sized Lazzaroni Amaretti di Saronno, at least for the top layer.

Serves 8–10

chocolate and almond
refrigerator cake

Star anise, a spice native to China, adds an exotic note that complements the other rich flavours of this dessert.

chocolate star anise cake with coffee caramel cream

200 g (7 oz/1⅓ cups) roughly chopped good-quality dark chocolate
125 g (4½ oz/½ cup) unsalted butter
4 eggs
2 egg yolks
115 g (4 oz/½ cup) caster (superfine) sugar
50 g (1¾ oz/heaped ⅓ cup) plain (all-purpose) flour, sifted
2 teaspoons ground star anise
50 g (1¾ oz/½ cup) ground almonds

coffee caramel cream
125 ml (4 fl oz/½ cup) thick (double/heavy) cream
3 tablespoons soft brown sugar
2 tablespoons brewed espresso coffee, cooled

Preheat the oven to 190ºC (375ºF/Gas 5). Grease and line a 23 cm (9 inch) round springform cake tin.

Put the chocolate and butter in a bowl set over a saucepan of gently simmering water, making sure the base of the bowl does not touch the water. Heat gently until the mixture is melted.

Put the eggs, egg yolks and sugar into a bowl and beat with electric beaters for 5 minutes until thickened. Fold in the flour, ground star anise and ground almonds and then fold in the melted chocolate mixture until evenly combined (the mixture should be runny at this stage).

Pour the mixture into the prepared tin and bake for 30–35 minutes, or until a skewer inserted in the middle comes out clean. Cool in the tin for 5 minutes and then remove and cool on a wire rack.

To make the coffee caramel cream, whip the cream, sugar and coffee together until soft peaks form and the colour is a soft caramel. Serve the cold cake cut into wedges with a spoonful of the coffee caramel cream.

Serves 8

Muscovado sugar, a soft, sticky, partially refined sugar, gives
a distinctive caramel taste to the topping on this torte.

chocolate and carrot torte with muscovado cream

185 g (6^1/$_2$ oz/1 cup) raw caster
(superfine) sugar
300 g (10^1/$_2$ oz/2 cups) grated
carrot (2 large carrots)
185 g (6^1/$_2$ oz/1^1/$_2$ cups) self-
raising flour
2 tablespoons unsweetened
cocoa powder
2 teaspoons ground cinnamon
2 eggs, lightly beaten
3 tablespoons light olive oil
3 tablespoons pouring
(whipping) cream or
buttermilk

100 g (3^1/$_2$ oz/heaped ^{3}/$_4$ cup)
grated dark chocolate
90 g (3^1/$_4$ oz/^{3}/$_4$ cup) chopped
pecans

topping
250 ml (9 fl oz/1 cup) thickened
(whipping) cream
1 teaspoon caster (superfine)
sugar
4 tablespoons thick Greek-style
yoghurt
^{1}/$_4$ teaspoom rum
2–3 tablespoons dark
muscovado (Barbados) or
dark brown sugar

Preheat the oven to 180°C (350°F/Gas4). Grease a 20 cm (8 inch) round springform cake tin and line the base with baking paper. Put the sugar and carrot in a large bowl and mix lightly.

Sift in the flour, cocoa and cinnamon, then add the eggs, olive oil and cream. Stir with a wooden spoon for about 30 seconds, or until combined. Fold in the chocolate and pecans. Pour into the tin and bake for 35–40 minutes, or until a skewer comes out clean when inserted in the centre. Cool in the tin for 5 minutes before turning out onto a wire rack to cool completely.

Make the topping 2–3 hours before serving. Whip the cream until stiff peaks form, incorporating the caster sugar, yoghurt and rum towards the end. Spread over the top of the cake and sprinkle the muscovado sugar over the top. Leave in a cool spot and allow the sugar to melt into a syrup. Cut into slices to serve.

Serves 8

chocolate and carrot torte with
muscovado cream

chocolate ricotta layer cake

125 g (4¹/2 oz/¹/2 cup) butter
150 g (5¹/2 oz/²/3 cup) sugar
1 teaspoon natural vanilla
    extract
2 eggs, lightly beaten
80 g (2³/4 oz/¹/4 cup) raspberry
    jam
150 g (5¹/2 oz/1¹/4 cups) self-
    raising flour
60 g (2¹/4 oz/¹/2 cup)
    unsweetened cocoa powder
1 teaspoon bicarbonate of soda
250 ml (9 fl oz/1 cup) milk

sugar syrup
2 tablespoons sugar
2 tablespoons Drambuie liqueur

ricotta filling
250 g (9 oz/1 cup) ricotta cheese
2 tablespoons caster (superfine)
    sugar
2 tablespoons Drambuie liqueur

60 g (2¹/4 oz/¹/4 cup) glacé
    (candied) figs or apricots,
    chopped
60 g (2¹/4 oz/¹/4 cup) glacé
    (candied) cherries, chopped
2 tablespoons chopped glacé
    (candied) ginger pieces
50 g (1³/4 oz/¹/3 cup) finely
    chopped dark chocolate
125 ml (4 fl oz/¹/2 cup)
    thickened (whipping) cream,
    whipped to firm peaks

chocolate buttercream
125 g (4¹/2 oz/heaped ³/4 cup)
    chopped dark chocolate
125 g (4¹/2 oz /¹/2 cup) butter,
    chopped
85 g (3 oz/²/3 cup) icing
    (confectioners') sugar

45 g (1¹/2 oz/¹/2 cup) flaked
    almonds, toasted

Preheat the oven to 180°C (350°F/Gas 4). Grease a 22 cm (8 1/2 inch) round cake tin and line the base with baking paper. Using electric beaters, beat the butter, sugar and vanilla in a small bowl until creamy. Add the eggs one at a time, beating well. Beat in the jam. Transfer the mixture to a larger bowl. Fold in the combined sifted flour, cocoa powder and bicarbonate of soda alternately with the milk. Pour into the tin. Bake for about 45 minutes, or until cooked when tested with a skewer. Leave in the tin for 15 minutes, then turn out onto a wire rack to cool.

For the sugar syrup, put the sugar and 3 tablespoons water in a small saucepan. Stir to dissolve, then bring to the boil over medium heat. Boil for 1 minute, remove from heat and stir in the liqueur. Set aside. For the ricotta filling, beat together the ricotta, caster sugar and liqueur until smooth. Stir in the fruit and chocolate. Fold in the whipped cream; refrigerate. For the chocolate buttercream, melt the chocolate, then set aside to cool. In a small bowl, beat the butter and icing sugar with electric beaters until creamy. Beat in the cooled chocolate until thick and creamy.

To assemble, cut the cake into three layers. Put one layer on a serving plate; brush with some of the sugar syrup. Spread with half the ricotta filling. Top with another cake layer, brush with syrup and spread with the remaining ricotta filling. Brush the cut underside of the third cake layer with the remaining syrup and place, cut side down, on top. Spread the chocolate buttercream all over the cake. Sprinkle the top with the almonds. Refrigerate for at least 1 hour before serving.

Serves 8–10

chocolate and chestnut marquis loaf

125 g (4^1/$_2$ oz/heaped ^{3}/$_4$ cup) chopped dark chocolate
110 g (3^3/$_4$ oz) chestnut purée, finely grated
1 tablespoon brandy
50 g (1^3/$_4$ oz) butter
2 tablespoons unsweetened cocoa powder
3 tablespoons caster (superfine) sugar
2 egg yolks

1 teaspoon powdered gelatine
170 ml (5^1/$_2$ fl oz/^{2}/$_3$ cup) thickened (whipping) cream

fresh raspberries, to serve
icing (confectioners') sugar, to dust

Line a 6 x 17 cm (2^1/$_2$ x 6^1/$_2$ inch) loaf or bar tin with plastic wrap. Leave some overhang to assist with turning out. Melt the chocolate in a small heatproof bowl over a saucepan of simmering water, making sure that the base of the bowl does not touch the water, stirring frequently. Remove from the heat and stir in the grated chestnut and brandy. Allow to cool.

In a bowl, using electric beaters, beat the butter, cocoa and half the sugar until creamy.

In a separate small bowl, using electric beaters, beat the egg yolks and remaining sugar until creamy.

Put the gelatine in a small bowl with 2 teaspoons water. Set over a basin of hot water to dissolve the gelatine. In another bowl, beat the cream until firm, then set aside.

Using electric beaters, beat the cooled chocolate and chestnut mixture into the butter mixture until smooth. Fold in the egg mixture and gelatine, then finally fold in the beaten cream.

Pour the mixture into the prepared tin. Cover with the overlapping plastic and refrigerate for several hours or overnight.

To serve, remove the marquis from the tin with the aid of the plastic wrap. Using a hot knife, cut into thick slices while cold and put onto serving plates. Dust the raspberries with icing sugar and serve to the side.

Serves 10–12

chocolate and chestnut
marquis loaf

Try these lightly baked puddings with their molten chocolate centres for a sophisticated, adult take on comfort food.

baked chocolate puddings with rich chocolate sauce

1½ tablespoons unsweetened cocoa powder, sifted
150 g (5½ oz/1 cup) chopped good-quality dark chocolate
120 g (4¼ oz/½ cup) unsalted butter, softened
3 eggs, at room temperature
2 egg yolks, at room temperature
55 g (2 oz/¼ cup) caster (superfine) sugar

90 g (3¼ oz/¾ cup) plain (all-purpose) flour

chocolate sauce
80 g (2¾ oz/½ cup) chopped good-quality dark chocolate
125 ml (4 fl oz/½ cup) pouring (whipping) cream

Preheat the oven to 180°C (350°F/Gas 4). Grease six 125 ml (4 fl oz/ ½ cup) metal dariole moulds and line the bottoms of each with a circle of baking paper. Dust the moulds with the cocoa powder.

Put the chocolate in a small heatproof bowl set over a small saucepan of simmering water, making sure the base of the bowl doesn't touch the water. Allow the chocolate to melt, then add the butter. When the butter has melted, stir to combine, then remove from the heat.

Beat the eggs, egg yolks and sugar in a large bowl with electric beaters until thick, creamy and pale. Gently fold in the chocolate mixture. Sift in the flour and gently fold through. Spoon the mixture into the moulds, leaving about 1 cm ($1/2$ inch) at the top of the moulds to allow the puddings to rise. Bake for 10 minutes, or until the top is firm and risen.

Meanwhile, for the chocolate sauce, put the chocolate and cream in a small heatproof bowl and set over a small saucepan of simmering water, making sure the base of the bowl doesn't touch the water. Stir until melted and combined.

To serve, run a knife around the moulds to loosen the puddings, then carefully turn them out onto serving plates. Drizzle with the sauce and serve immediately.

Serves 6

profiteroles with coffee mascarpone and dark chocolate sauce

125 g (4^1/$_2$ oz/1 cup) plain
  (all-purpose) flour
70 g (2^1/$_2$ oz) unsalted butter,
  cubed
^{1}/$_2$ teaspoon salt
4 eggs, at room temperature

filling
2 tablespoons instant coffee
  granules
450 g (1 lb/2 cups) mascarpone
  cheese

2 tablespoons icing
  (confectioners') sugar

chocolate sauce
100 g (3^1/$_2$ oz/^{2}/$_3$ cup) good-
  quality chopped dark
  chocolate
1^1/$_2$ tablespoons unsalted butter
80 ml (2^1/$_2$ fl oz/^{1}/$_3$ cup) pouring
  (whipping) cream

Preheat the oven to 200°C (400°F/Gas 6). Lightly grease two baking trays. Sift the flour onto a piece of baking paper. Put the butter, salt and 250 ml (9 fl oz/1 cup) water in a saucepan and bring to a boil, stirring occasionally. Using the baking paper as a funnel, quickly pour the flour into the boiling mixture. Reduce the heat to low, then beat vigorously with a wooden spoon until the mixture leaves the side of the pan and forms a smooth ball. Transfer the mixture to a bowl and set aside to cool until lukewarm. Using electric beaters, beat in the eggs, one at a time, until the mixture is thick and glossy.

Using two spoons, gently drop 16 rounded balls of the mixture about 3 cm (1¼ inches) in diameter and 3 cm (1¼ inches) apart onto the prepared baking sheets. Bake for 20 minutes, or until the balls are puffed. Reduce the oven to 180°C (350°F/Gas 4) and bake for 10 minutes more, or until the puffs are golden brown and crisp.

Using a small sharp knife, gently slit the puffs to allow the steam to escape, then return them to the oven for 10 minutes, or until the insides are dry. Cool to room temperature.

Meanwhile, to make the filling, dissolve the instant coffee in 1 tablespoon boiling water. Set aside to cool. Stir together the coffee, mascarpone and sugar until just combined. Be careful not to overmix, or the mascarpone mixture will separate.

To make the bittersweet chocolate sauce, put the chocolate, butter and cream in a small heatproof bowl set over a small saucepan of simmering water, making sure the base of the bowl doesn't touch the water. Stir until combined. Set aside to cool slightly.

Just before serving, slit the profiteroles in half and sandwich together with the filling. Drizzle with the chocolate sauce, or serve the sauce separately.

Makes 16

profiteroles with coffee mascarpone
and dark chocolate sauce

chocolate, hazelnut and orange dessert cake with blood-orange sauce

200 g (7 oz/1¹/₃ cups) good-quality chopped dark chocolate

200 g (7 oz/1¹/₂ cups) blanched hazelnuts

200 g (7 oz) unsalted butter, softened

125 g (4¹/₂ oz/²/₃ cup) raw caster (superfine) sugar

4 eggs, at room temperature, separated

3 teaspoons espresso instant coffee granules

finely grated zest of 1 orange

100 g (3¹/₂ oz/heaped ³/₄ cup) cornflour (cornstarch)

icing (confectioners') sugar, to dust

thick (double/heavy) cream, to serve

blood-orange syrup

250 ml (9 fl oz/1 cup) strained blood-orange juice (from 4–5 oranges)

55 g (2 oz/¹/₄ cup) caster (superfine) sugar

1 teaspoon orange liqueur such as Cointreau (optional)

Preheat the oven to 170°C (325°F/Gas 3). Grease a 21 cm (8¹/₄ inch) round springform cake tin.

Put the chocolate in a heatproof bowl set over a saucepan of simmering water, making sure the base of the bowl doesn't touch the water. Heat, stirring, until melted.

Put the hazelnuts in a food processor and process until finely chopped. Cream the butter and caster sugar in a large bowl with electric beaters until pale and fluffy. Add the egg yolks, one at a time, beating well after each addition. Gently stir in the melted chocolate, coffee granules and orange zest. Mix in the cornflour and chopped hazelnuts.

Whisk the egg whites until soft peaks form. Using a large metal spoon, fold a scoop of egg white into the chocolate mixture Gently fold in the remaining egg white. Spoon the mixture into the prepared tin and level the surface. Bake for 30 minutes, then cover loosely with foil and bake for another 40–45 minutes, or until a skewer inserted into the centre of the cake comes out clean. Don't be too concerned if the surface cracks.

Meanwhile, for the blood-orange syrup, put the orange juice and sugar in a small saucepan and stir over low heat until the sugar has dissolved. Bring to the boil, then reduce the heat and simmer for 10–12 minutes, or until reduced by about half. Stir in the liqueur, if using, and set aside to cool slightly.

To serve, cut the warm cake into slices. Lightly dust with confectioners' sugar, spoon over a little of the warm orange syrup, and serve with cream.

Serves 6–8

black and white chocolate tart

pastry

90 g (3^1/4 oz) unsalted butter, at room temperature

55 g (2 oz/^{1}/4 cup) caster (superfine) sugar

1 egg, at room temperature, lightly beaten

185 g (6^1/2 oz/1^1/2 cups) plain (all-purpose) flour

30 g (1 oz/^{1}/4 cup) self-raising flour

1 tablespoon cocoa powder

filling

2 teaspoons powdered gelatine

200 ml (7 fl oz) milk

115 (4 oz/^{1}/2 cup) caster (superfine) sugar

80 g (2^3/4 oz/^{1}/2 cup) chopped good-quality white chocolate

4 egg yolks, at room temperature, lightly beaten

240 ml (8 fl oz) thickened (whipping) cream, whipped to soft peaks

chocolate glaze

60 ml (2 fl oz/^{1}/4 cup) pouring (whipping) cream

80 g (2^3/4 oz/^{1}/2 cup) chopped good-quality dark chocolate

2 teaspoons unsalted butter, cubed

2 teaspoons liquid glucose

Preheat the oven to 190°C (375°F/Gas 5). Lightly grease the sides of a 21 cm (8^1/4 inch) springform cake tin and line the base with baking paper.

For the pastry, beat the butter with an electric beater until smooth and fluffy. Beat in the sugar and egg until combined. Sift in the combined flours and cocoa and stir until the dough comes together. Knead briefly on a lightly floured surface until smooth. Flatten into a disk, wrap in plastic wrap, and refrigerate for 30 minutes. Roll the pastry between two sheets of baking paper until about 8 mm (3/8 inch) thick, and trim to fit the base of the tin. Ease the pastry into the tin, removing the paper, and lightly prick with a fork. Bake for 15 minutes, or until slightly firm to the touch. Set aside to cool.

For the filling, combine the gelatine and 2 tablespoons water in a small bowl and set aside for 2 minutes to sponge and swell. Heat the milk, sugar and chocolate in a saucepan until simmering. Stir until the sugar has dissolved and the chocolate has melted. Put the egg yolks in a bowl and whisk in the warm chocolate mixture. Return the mixture to a clean saucepan and stir over medium heat until it lightly coats the back of a spoon. Add the sponged gelatine and stir until dissolved. Transfer to a bowl, place over a bowl of ice and beat until cold. Fold in the cream. Pour the mixture over the pastry and refrigerate overnight, or until set.

For the glaze, put the cream, chocolate, butter and glucose in a saucepan and stir over low–medium heat until smooth. Cool until thickened. Remove the pie from the tin and spoon the glaze over the top, allowing it to drip down the sides. Use a metal spatula to smooth the glaze over the top of the tart. Set aside at room temperature for 1 hour, or until the glaze is set.

Serves 12

black and white chocolate tart

Self-saucing puddings are a little bit of kitchen magic: the sauce goes in on the top but — hey presto!— ends up on the bottom.

chocolate and cinnamon self-saucing puddings

50 g (1³/4 oz/¹/3 cup) chopped
   good-quality dark chocolate
60 g (2¹/4 oz/¹/4 cup) unsalted
   butter, cubed
2 tablespoons unsweetened
   cocoa powder, sifted
160 ml (5¹/4 fl oz) milk
125 g (4¹/2 oz/1 cup) self-raising
   flour
115 g (4 oz/¹/2 cup) caster
   (superfine) sugar
80 g (2³/4 oz/¹/3 cup firmly
   packed) soft brown sugar

1 egg, at room temperature,
   lightly beaten
thick (double/heavy) cream,
   to serve

cinnamon sauce
1¹/2 teaspoons ground
   cinnamon
50 g (1³/4 oz) unsalted butter,
   cubed
60 g (2¹/4 oz/¹/4 cup firmly
   packed) soft brown sugar
30 g (1 oz/¹/4 cup)
   unsweetended cocoa
   powder, sifted

Preheat the oven to 180°C (350°F/Gas 4). Grease four 250 ml (9 fl oz/ 1 cup) ovenproof ramekins.

Combine the chocolate, butter, cocoa and milk in a saucepan. Stir over low heat until the chocolate has melted. Remove from the heat.

Sift the flour into a large bowl and stir in the sugars. Add to the chocolate mixture with the egg and mix well. Spoon the mixture into the prepared dishes, put on a baking sheet and set aside while you make the sauce.

For the cinnamon sauce, combine the cinnamon, butter, brown sugar, cocoa and 375 ml (13 fl oz/1^1/2 cups) water in a small saucepan. Stir over low heat until combined. Carefully pour the sauce onto the puddings over the back of a spoon. Bake for 40 minutes, or until firm. Turn out the puddings and serve with heavy cream.

Serves 4

chocolate ravioli

filling

60 g (2¼ oz) good-quality dark
   chocolate (60% cocoa solids),
   chopped
30 g (1 oz) unsalted butter,
   cubed
45 ml (1½ fl oz) pouring
   (whipping) cream

dough

250 g (9 oz/2 cups) plain
   (all-purpose) flour
½ teaspoon baking powder

2 teaspoons caster (superfine)
   sugar
¼ teaspoon salt
1 egg
100 ml (3½ fl oz) light olive oil
2½ tablespoons dry white wine

1 egg, lightly beaten
vegetable oil, for deep-frying
icing (confectioners') sugar, to
   dust
125 ml (4 fl oz/½ cup) maple
   syrup, to serve (optional)

For the filling, melt the chocolate, butter and cream in a small bowl set over a saucepan of simmering water, making sure the base of the bowl does not touch the water. Stir until smooth and glossy. Remove the bowl from the heat, cool and refrigerate until solid.

For the dough, put the flour, baking powder, sugar and salt in a food processor and pulse until just combined. Mix together the egg, olive oil and wine in a jug. Gradually pour into the processor while the motor is running, then stop processing when the mixture starts to clump together.

Transfer to a lightly floured surface and knead for 3–4 minutes until smooth and elastic. Cover with plastic wrap and refrigerate for 30 minutes.

Roll the dough out to 2–3 mm (^{1}/16–^{1}/8 inch) thickness. Cover with a tea towel (dish towel) and allow to rest while you shape the filling.

Using a teaspoon or a small melon baller, scoop out rounded teaspoonfuls of the chocolate filling. They don't need to be perfectly round, but in a solid lump. If the kitchen is hot, keep the balls in the refrigerator and take out a few at a time as needed. You will need 18 balls.

With a biscuit cutter or a glass, cut 8 cm (3^1/4 inch) rounds from the dough. Brush around the rims of a few rounds with a little beaten egg. Place a chocolate ball in the centre of each. Fold the dough over to encase it, forming a half-moon shape. Press the edges together firmly to seal. Put on a tray and refrigerate while you make the rest of the ravioli.

Half-fill a deep saucepan with oil and heat until hot but not smoking, about 180°C (350°F). Fry the ravioli, a few at a time, for 1^1/2 minutes, or until puffed and golden brown. Drain on scrunched-up paper towels then dust liberally with icing sugar. Serve warm while the chocolate centre is still melted, accompanied by a small bowl of maple syrup for dipping.

Makes 18

chocolate ravioli

This dark, dense, delectable cake is proof that the most delicious recipes need not be complicated.

dark chocolate pecan torte

300 g (10½ oz/3 cups) pecans
250 g (9 oz/1⅔ cups) chopped
   dark chocolate
300 g (10½ oz) butter, cubed
4 eggs, separated

230 g (8 oz/1 cup) caster
   (superfine) sugar
2 tablespoons brandy
whipped cream, to serve

Preheat the oven to 160°C (315°F/Gas 2–3). Grease a 25 cm (10 inch) springform cake tin and line the base with baking paper.

In a food processor, process the pecans until finely chopped. Heat the chocolate and butter in a bowl set over a saucepan of simmering water, making sure the base of the bowl does not touch the water. Stir until just melted. Set aside.

Using electric beaters, beat the egg yolks and sugar in a large bowl for about 2 minutes, until thick and pale. Slowly beat in the melted chocolate mixture, then use a metal spoon to fold in the pecans.

In a separate clean bowl, beat the egg whites to firm peaks. Fold in one-third of the egg white to loosen the mixture, then lightly fold in the remainder. Spoon into the prepared tin and smooth the surface. Bake for 10 minutes. Reduce the temperature to 150°C (300°F/Gas 2) and bake for 45 minutes more, or until set and firm to the touch. Sprinkle the brandy over the cake while it is still warm. Leave the cake to cool completely in the tin before removing.

Cut into wedges and serve warm, cold or chilled with whipped cream.

Serves 10–12

mocha lamingtons

125 g (4¹/2 oz) unsalted butter, chopped, softened
230 g (8 oz/1 cup) caster (superfine) sugar
¹/2 teaspoon natural vanilla extract
2 eggs
250 g (9 oz/2 cups) self-raising flour
250 ml (9 fl oz/1 cup) milk
2 teaspoons instant coffee granules, dissolved in 2 teaspoons boiling water

icing
375 g (13 oz/3 cups) icing (confectioners') sugar
60 g (2¹/4 oz/¹/2 cup) unsweetened cocoa powder
20 g (³/4 oz) unsalted butter
2 teaspoons instant coffee powder
75 g (2¹/2 oz/1¹/4 cups) shredded coconut
90 g (3¹/4 oz/1 cup) desiccated (dried grated) coconut

Preheat the oven to 180°C (350°F/Gas 4). Lightly grease the base of a 23 cm (9 inch) square shallow tin and line the base with baking paper.

Cream the butter, sugar and vanilla in a bowl using electric beaters until pale and fluffy. Add the eggs one at a time, beating well after each addition. Sift the flour into a bowl, then stir the flour into the butter mixture alternately with the milk until combined and smooth. Spoon half the mixture into the prepared tin and spread evenly over the base. Add the dissolved coffee to the remaining mixture and stir until well combined. Carefully spread the coffee mixture over the mixture in the tin.

Bake for 30–35 minutes, or until a skewer inserted into the centre of the cake comes out clean. Cool in the tin for 5 minutes before turning out onto a wire rack to cool. Cut into 25 squares.

To make the icing, sift the icing sugar and cocoa powder into a large shallow bowl. Add the butter and coffee and gradually whisk in 150 ml (5 fl oz) boiling water until smooth. Put the shredded and desiccated coconuts in a large shallow bowl and toss to combine.

Using two spoons to hold the cake, dip the cake squares into the icing to cover, allowing the excess to drip off. (Add a little boiling water to the icing if it starts to thicken). Roll the cake in the coconut to cover and place on a wire rack. Repeat with the remaining cakes.

Makes 25

dreamy and creamy Smooth, silky and delicately pretty, these desserts hark back to a time when life was a little less rushed, and meals a little less expedient; when eating wasn't a matter of wolfing down a meal, then rushing off, but lingering over good conversation and a last, indulgent spoonful of a home-made creamy treat. Here, you can rediscover those dreamy days indeed.

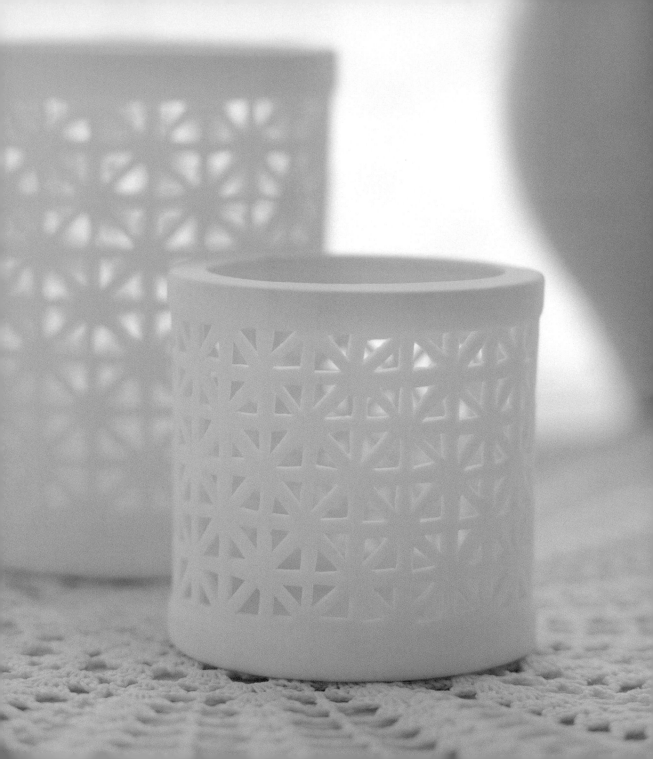

Double cream, whipping cream, custard, cream cheese, panna cotta, mascarpone, crème fraîche, crème anglaise — the list could go on! Cream in all its glorious forms and creations is the star of this chapter. From the classic heart-shaped dessert coeur a la crème to rich mocha coffee cream pots and fragrant panna cotta filo with rosewater syrup and pistachios, cream has been adding a touch of luxury to desserts and cakes for a very long, happy time. Unlike the boldness of chocolate desserts or the fresh vitality of fruit-based sweets, creamy concoctions invite a more gentle, unhurried approach to cooking and sharing food. For the cook, there is pleasure to be found in the presentation of such pretty desserts — lace and filigree, the good glassware and pressed linen napkins all seem to be required. And for the lucky diner, certainly, it's hard to rush off when faced with the silky seductiveness of a crème caramel or a cardamom kulfi. Appropriately for such a well-loved ingredient, this chapter contains many familiar recipes such as lemon tart and tiramisù, as well as many contemporary recipes, such as honeycomb and mascarpone cheesecake. Creamy desserts are defined by their all-together too-smooth texture. Yet if textures are wonderfully uniform, flavours are surprisingly varied. Honey, coffee, alcohol, fruit and nuts, as well as spices and perfumes such as vanilla, cinnamon, ginger and flower waters, all add depth and flavour to these desserts. Sophisticated, subtle, festive — cream truly deserves its place at the heart of many classic recipes. Who wouldn't linger over such desserts?

coeur à la crème with blueberry coulis

250 g (9 oz/1 cup) farm cheese
  or Neufchatel
60 g (2¼ oz/½ cup) icing
  (confectioners') sugar
¼ teaspoon natural vanilla
  extract
250 ml (9 oz/1 cup) thickened
  (whipping) cream

blueberry coulis
150 g (5½ oz/1 cup) fresh
  blueberries
1 tablespoon caster (superfine)
  sugar

1 teaspoon lemon juice
1 teaspoon crème de cassis
  (blackcurrant liqueur)
  (optional)

sugared fruits
1 small bunch each green and
  purple seedless grapes
  (about 25 grapes) (see Note)
2 egg whites, lightly whisked
55 g (2 oz/¼ cup) caster
  (superfine) sugar

Line one large or four individual coeur a la crème moulds (see Note) with muslin (cheesecloth). Put the cheese, icing sugar and vanilla in a food processor and process until smooth. In a large bowl, whip the cream until firm peaks form. Fold the cheese mixture through the cream.

Spoon the mixture into the prepared mould and pack down tightly. Cover the mould and stand it on a shallow dish. Put in the refrigerator and leave for 12 hours or overnight to drain.

For the blueberry coulis, process the blueberries and sugar in a food processor until smooth and glossy. Strain through a fine sieve into a jug, pressing the pulp through. Stir in the lemon juice and liqueur.

For the sugared fruits, brush each piece with egg white. While still wet, dip into the sugar and put on a tray lined with baking paper to dry.

To serve, unmould the coeur(s) onto a serving plate and gently peel off the muslin. Spoon a little coulis over and around each and pile the sugared fruits on top.

Notes: Coeur à la crème moulds are heart shaped, with holes in the base to allow for drainage of the liquid (whey) from the cheese mixture with which they are filled. If you can't obtain a large mould, use four individual ones. Choose small grapes for decoration so that they don't dwarf the dessert. When available, fresh black or white currants in little bunches also work well.

Serves 4

meringue sandwiches with passionfruit cream and raspberries

2 egg whites
250 g (9 oz/heaped 1 cup) caster
   (superfine) sugar
1/2 teaspoon natural vanilla
   extract
1/2 teaspoon cornflour
   (cornstarch)

passionfruit cream
125 ml (4 fl oz/1/2 cup)
   thickened (whipping) cream
4 tablespoons passionfruit pulp
   (from 2 large passionfruit)

macadamia toffee shards
50 g (13/4 oz/1/3 cup) roasted
   unsalted macadamia nuts
90 g (31/4 oz/heaped 1/3 cup)
   caster (superfine) sugar

passionfruit liqueur sauce
3 tablespoons strained
   passionfruit juice (from
   6 large passionfruit)
1 tablespoon caster (superfine)
   sugar
2 teaspoons cornflour
   (cornstarch)
1 tablespoon Grand Marnier
   or other orange liqueur

125 ml (4 fl oz/1/2 cup)
   thickened (whipping) cream,
   extra
1 tablespoon icing
   (confectioners') sugar
50 g (13/4 oz/scant 1/2 cup) fresh
   raspberries

Preheat the oven to 130°C (250°F/Gas 1). Line a large baking tray with baking paper. Beat the egg whites with electric beaters until firm peaks form. Gradually add the sugar. Beat for 3 minutes, until the sugar has dissolved and the meringue is glossy and thick. Beat in the vanilla and cornflour. Put eight spoonfuls evenly spaced onto the tray and flatten slightly to form an 8 cm (3¼ inch) freeform circle. Bake for about 40 minutes, until crisp on the outside. Turn off the oven and with the door ajar, leave the meringues in the oven to cool.

For the passionfruit cream, whip the cream in a small bowl until firm peaks form. Fold in the passionfruit pulp until smooth. Chill. For the toffee, roughly chop the macadamias and put on a lightly greased tray. Put the sugar and 3 tablespoons water in a saucepan. Stir until the sugar dissolves, then increase the heat. Boil, without stirring, for 4–5 minutes, or until the mixture caramelizes. Pour over the nuts and leave to harden. Break into pieces and store in an airtight container until needed.

For the sauce, combine the passionfruit juice, sugar and cornflour in a small saucepan. Stir over low heat until thickened. Remove from the heat and stir in the liqueur. Set aside but do not refrigerate. Whip the extra cream with the 1 tablespoon icing sugar until thick.

To assemble, put four meringues onto serving plates. Spread the passion-fruit cream over each. Top with the remaining meringues, then the whipped cream, passionfruit liqueur sauce and a few raspberries. Decorate each sandwich with a shard of toffee and serve immediately.

Serves 4

meringue sandwiches with passionfruit
cream and raspberries

mocha coffee cream pots

festive cannoli

For a really good chocolate sauce, use fine-quality chocolate with 50–70 per cent cocoa solids.

coffee crémets with chocolate sauce

250 g (9 oz/1 cup) cream cheese
250 ml (9 oz/1 cup) thick
   (double/heavy) cream
4 tablespoons very strong coffee
80 g (2³/4 oz/¹/3 cup) caster
   (superfine) sugar

chocolate sauce
100 g (3¹/2 oz) dark chocolate
50 g (1³/4 oz) unsalted butter

Line four 100 ml (3¹/2 fl oz) ramekins with plastic wrap, leaving enough hanging over the side to wrap over the crémet. Beat the cream cheese a little until smooth, then whisk in the cream. Mix in the coffee and sugar. Spoon into the ramekins and fold the plastic wrap over the top. Refrigerate for at least 1¹/2 hours, then unwrap, turn the crémets out onto serving plates, and carefully peel off the plastic wrap.

For the sauce, gently melt the chocolate, butter and 4 tablespoons water in a saucepan. Stir well until shiny, then let the sauce cool a little. Pour a little chocolate sauce over each crémet.

Serves 4

cardamom and yoghurt bavarois

4 egg yolks
115 g (4 oz/1/2 cup) caster
    (superfine) sugar
200 g (7 oz) vanilla yoghurt
185 ml (6 fl oz/3/4 cup) milk

1 teaspoon ground cardamom
1/2 teaspoon vanilla extract
1 tablespoon powdered gelatine
300 ml (101/2 fl oz) thickened
    (whipping) cream

Beat the egg yolks and sugar until thick and pale. Combine the yoghurt, milk, cardamom and vanilla in a saucepan and stir over low heat until just coming to the simmer. Pour the warm milk mixture over the yolks and whisk to combine. Return to a clean saucepan and stir over medium heat for 7–8 minutes, or until the custard has thickened enough to coat the back of a wooden spoon. Remove from the heat.

Dissolve the gelatine in 3 tablespoons of hot water and stir it through the custard. Set the custard aside to cool completely. Whip the cream until soft peaks form, then gently fold the cream through the cooled custard.

Divide the mixture among eight 125 ml (4 fl oz/1/2 cup) moulds and refrigerate for 2–3 hours to set. To unmould, dip a blunt knife into warm water and run the tip around the edge of the mould. Dip the mould into a bowl of warm water for a few seconds, shaking slightly to loosen. Place the serving plate over the mould, invert and remove the mould.

Makes 8

passionfruit swirl cheesecake gateau

pecan bavarian with baileys cream

coconut and ginger
crème brulée

stem ginger cheesecake with
sauternes poached plums

coconut bavarian cream with papaya,
pineapple and lychee

custard tarts with rhubarb

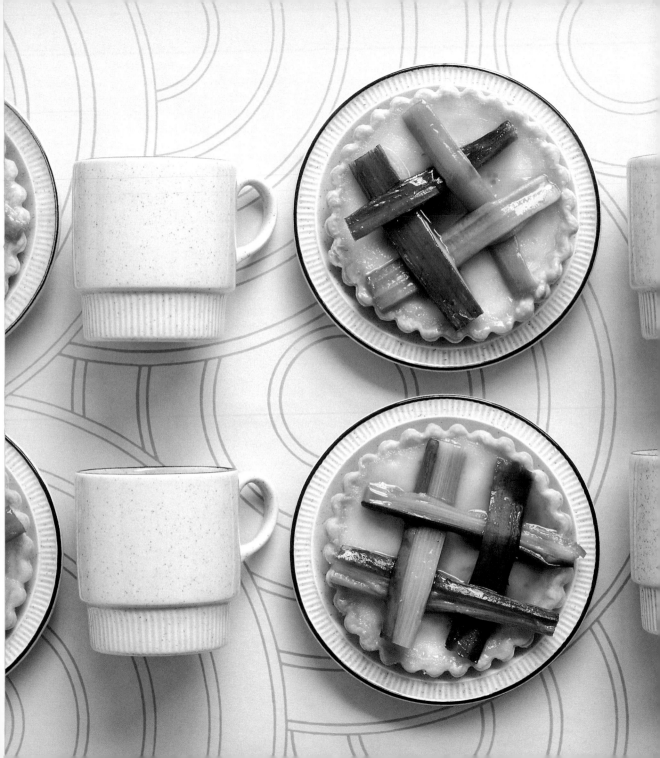

honey parfait with caramelized
cumquats

Fragile-looking filo pastry is surprisingly hardy. As you work, cover the sheets with a clean damp cloth to keep them pliable.

vanilla custard log

750 ml (26 fl oz/3 cups) milk
50 g (1³/4 oz/heaped ¹/3 cup)
    cornflour (cornstarch)
1 vanilla bean
6 egg yolks, at room
    temperature
150 g (5¹/2 oz/²/3 cup) caster
    (superfine) sugar

2¹/2 tablespoons finely grated
    orange zest
8 sheets filo pastry
40 g (1¹/2 oz) ghee or unsalted
    butter, melted

icing (confectioners') sugar,
    to dust

Combine 60 ml (2 fl oz/¹/4 cup) of the milk with the cornflour and mix to a paste. Put the remaining milk in a saucepan over medium heat. Split the vanilla bean lengthways and scrape the seeds into the pan, discarding the pod. Add the cornflour paste, egg yolks, caster sugar and orange zest and whisk to combine. Boil, stirring, for 4 minutes, or until the custard is very thick. Remove from the heat, cover the surface with plastic wrap and set aside to cool.

Preheat the oven to 180°C (350°F/Gas 4). Line a baking tray with baking paper. Brush a sheet of filo pastry with the melted ghee or butter. Top with a second sheet of filo, brush with ghee or butter, then repeat with two more sheets of pastry. Make another stack of four sheets of pastry in the same way.

Spoon half the custard along the long edge of one rectangle of pastry, leaving a 9 cm (3 1/2 inch) border, and shape into a 30 cm (12 inch) log. Carefully lift the border side of the pastry over the custard and roll up, tucking under the sides as you roll. Repeat with the remaining custard and pastry to make a second log.

Place the rolls on the prepared tray and brush with melted ghee or butter. Bake for 20 minutes, or until golden. Do not overcook the rolls or the custard will leak. Set aside to cool for 10 minutes. Dust with plenty of icing sugar before serving.

Serves 8–10

fruity indulgences Versatile, colourful and full of flavour, fruit is the dessert world's most reliable participant. From breakfast and brunch to lunch, afternoon tea, snack time, dinner and cocktail hour, there isn't an occasion when the delicious goodness of fresh fruit isn't welcome. And the good news for busy cooks: sometimes the simplest things really are the best.

Bright berries; fragrant, tangy citrus; sweet, luscious stone fruit; juicy, exuberant tropical fruit: for an everyday staple, fruit has a lot to offer. Be it a family lunch or when friends stay for dinner, if you have some fruit in the fridge, sugar in the cupboard and you can snaffle some wine from the table, you can pretty much guarantee a tasty dessert. For this is surely one of the reasons why fruit has such enduring appeal: it requires very little effort to be transformed into a truly superb dessert. So while no one denies the value of the classic standby, the fruit platter, the recipes in this chapter demonstrate just how impressively easy it is to create something more spectacular. Fig and raspberry cake, Cointreau-glazed peaches and mixed berry sundae require neither unusual ingredients nor hours in the kitchen. What quickly becomes obvious is that with when cleverly combined with such flavours as chocolate, wine and honey, caramel or butterscotch sauce, the humble apple, pliant peach or everyday lemon becomes a bit of a wonder by the time it lands on the table. Depending on the fruit you have, you can create desserts that range in taste from tangy and cleansing to smooth and sweet, or rich and decadent. So can we be surprised to discover that after starting out as young children eating puréed apple and pear swirl, we eventually return not far from where we began; happily fighting over the last spoonful of mango fool or Eton mess? Fruit endures.

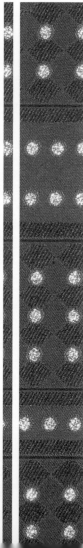

Named for the English college where it was created, this dessert is simplicity itself, yet rich enough to satisfy any sweet tooth.

eton mess

4–6 large ready-made
  meringues
250 g (9 oz/1²/₃ cups)
  strawberries (see Note)

1 teaspoon caster (superfine)
  sugar
250 ml (9 fl oz/1 cup) thick
  (double/heavy) cream

Break the meringues into pieces. Cut the strawberries into quarters and put them in a bowl with the sugar. Using a potato masher or the back of a spoon, squash them slightly so they start to become juicy. Whip the cream with a balloon or electric whisk until it is quite thick but not solid. Gently mix everything together and spoon it into pretty serving glasses. Serve immediately.

Note: Strawberries are traditionally used in this dish, but other berries may be substituted. Or, for a tropical version, use small chunks of mango, banana, papaya and/or pineapple, topped with fresh passionfruit pulp.

Serves 4

fig and raspberry cake

185 g (6¹/2 oz/³/4 cup) unsalted
butter
185 g (6¹/2 oz/heaped ³/4 cup)
caster (superfine) sugar,
plus extra for sprinkling
1 egg, plus 1 egg yolk

335 g (11³/4 oz/2²/3 cups) plain
(all-purpose) flour
1 teaspoon baking powder
4 fresh figs, quartered
grated zest of 1 orange
200 g (7 oz/1²/3 cups) raspberries
sugar, to sprinkle

Preheat the oven to 180°C (350°F/Gas 4). Lightly grease a 23 cm (9 inch) round springform cake tin. Cream the butter and sugar until pale. Add the egg and yolk and beat again. Sift in the flour, baking powder and a pinch of salt, and combine to form a dough. Chill until firm.

Divide the dough in two and roll out one piece until large enough to cover the base of the tin. Transfer it to the prepared tin and set in place, pressing the dough up the sides a little. Cover with the figs, orange zest and raspberries. Roll out the remaining dough and place it over the filling. Brush with water and sprinkle with a little sugar. Bake for 30 minutes, then serve warm.

Serves 6

Prescribed in medieval times as medicine, possets have now evolved into desserts—but they will still make you feel better.

lemon posset

110 g (3³/4 oz/¹/2 cup) caster (superfine) sugar

310 ml (10³/4 fl oz/1¹/4 cups) thick (double/heavy) cream

juice of 2 lemons (about 100 ml/ 3¹/2 fl oz)

wafer biscuits or tuiles, to serve

Place the sugar and cream in a saucepan over low heat and bring to the boil slowly, stirring so the sugar dissolves and the cream does not boil over. Boil for 2–3 minutes, then add the lemon juice and mix well.

Pour the mixture into four 100 ml (3¹/2 fl oz) ramekins, cover with plastic wrap and chill well for at least 2 hours, or overnight. Serve with biscuits such as wafers or tuiles.

Serves 4

peaches and raspberries cardinal

1 vanilla bean, split
230 g (8¼ oz/1 cup) caster
   (superfine) sugar
4 ripe peaches
350 g (12 oz/2¾ cups) fresh or
   thawed frozen raspberries
2 tablespoons icing
   (confectioners') sugar

2–3 tablespoons Curaçao or
   other orange liqueur
vanilla, boysenberry or
   raspberry ripple ice cream,
   to serve
35 g (1¼ oz/¼ cup) pistachio
   nuts, toasted, roughly
   chopped

Scrape the seeds from the vanilla bean. Put the seeds, the pod, the caster sugar and 750 ml (26 fl oz/3 cups) water in a large saucepan. Stir over low heat to dissolve the sugar. Bring to the boil, then reduce the heat to low and add the peaches. Simmer until tender, 4–6 minutes, depending on the ripeness of the fruit. Remove the peaches from the pan and when cool enough to handle, remove the skins. Leave the syrup to cool, then return the peaches to the syrup until ready to serve.

Reserve one-third of the raspberries. Purée the rest in a food processor with the icing sugar and Curaçao to taste. Sieve the purée and discard the seeds. To serve, put a peach in a glass dish and coat with a little of the reserved cooking syrup. Add a scoop of ice cream, a drizzle of raspberry sauce, a few reserved raspberries and scatter over the pistachios.

Serves 4

peaches and raspberries
cardinal

The harmonious trio of meringue, cream and berries has inspired many luscious desserts; this is perhaps the ultimate example.

classic pavlova

4 egg whites
230 g (8¼ oz/1 cup) caster (superfine) sugar
2 teaspoons cornflour (cornstarch)
1 teaspoon white vinegar

500 ml (17 fl oz/2 cups) thickened (whipping) cream
3 passionfruit, to decorate
250 g (9 oz) strawberries, to decorate

Preheat the oven to 160°C (315°F/Gas 2–3). Line a 32 x 28 cm (13 x 11 inch) baking tray with baking paper.

Place the egg whites and a pinch of salt in a small, dry bowl. Using electric beaters, beat until stiff peaks form. Add the sugar gradually, beating constantly after each addition, until the mixture is thick and glossy and all the sugar has dissolved.

Using a metal spoon, fold in the cornflour and vinegar. Spoon the mixture into a mound on the prepared tray. Lightly flatten the top of the pavlova and smooth the sides. It should be circular, and about 2.5 cm (1 in) high. Bake for 1 hour, or until pale cream and crisp. Remove from the oven while warm and carefully turn upside down onto a serving plate. Peel off the paper. Allow to cool, but do not refrigerate.

When ready to serve, lightly whip the cream until soft peaks form and spread it over the soft centre of the pavlova. Decorate with pulp from the passionfruit and halved strawberries. Cut into wedges to serve.

Note: While pavlovas are traditionally made with strawberries, other fresh berries may be used; or try banana slices and passionfruit pulp.

Serves 6–8

strawberries romanoff

750 g (1$\frac{1}{2}$ lb/5 cups)
 strawberries, quartered
2 tablespoons Cointreau or
 other orange liqueur
$\frac{1}{4}$ teaspoon finely grated
 orange zest

1 tablespoon caster (superfine)
 sugar
125 ml (4 fl oz/$\frac{1}{2}$ cup)
 thickened (whipping) cream
2 tablespoons icing
 (confectioners') sugar

Combine the strawberries, liqueur, zest and the caster sugar in a large bowl, cover and refrigerate for 1 hour. Drain the strawberries, reserving any juices. Purée about one-quarter of the berries with the reserved juices.

Divide the remaining berries among four pretty serving glasses. Beat the cream and icing sugar until soft peaks form, then fold the berry purée through the whipped cream. Spoon the mixture over the top of the strawberries, then cover and refrigerate until required.

Serves 4

mango fool

2 very ripe mangoes
80 ml (2¹/₂ fl oz/¹/₃ cup)
   thickened (whipping) cream

250 g (9 oz/1 cup) thick Greek-
   style yoghurt

Take the flesh off the mangoes. The easiest way to do this is to slice down either side of the stone so you have two 'cheeks'. Make crisscross cuts through the mango flesh on each cheek, almost through to the skin, then turn each cheek inside out and slice the flesh from the skin into a bowl. Cut the rest of the flesh from the stone.

Purée the flesh using a food processor or blender. Whip the cream until soft peaks form.

Put a spoonful of mango purée in the bottom of four small glasses, bowls or cups, put a spoonful of yoghurt on top and then repeat. When you have used up all the mango and yoghurt, spoon one-quarter of the cream over each serving. Swirl the layers together just before you eat them.

Serves 4

mango fool

The sharpness of rhubarb makes a tangy counterpoint for tender, sweet cake in this recipe suitable for an elegant afternoon tea.

rhubarb slice

300 g (10½ oz) rhubarb, trimmed and cut into 5 mm (¼ inch) thick slices

115 g (4 oz/½ cup) caster (superfine) sugar

185 g (6½ oz/¾ cup) unsalted butter, chopped

230 g (8 oz/1 cup) caster (superfine) sugar

½ teaspoon natural vanilla extract

3 eggs

90 g (3¼ oz/¾ cup) plain (all-purpose) flour

¾ teaspoon baking powder

1 tablespoon sugar

icing (confectioners') sugar, to dust

whipped or thick (double/heavy) cream, to serve

Combine the rhubarb and sugar in a bowl. Set aside for 1 hour, stirring occasionally, or until the rhubarb has released its juices and the sugar has dissolved. Strain well, discarding the liquid.

Preheat the oven to 180°C (350°F/Gas 4). Lightly grease a 20 x 30 cm (8 x 12 inch) rectangular shallow tin. Line the base with baking paper, leaving the paper hanging over the two long sides for easy removal later.

Cream the butter, sugar and vanilla in a bowl using electric beaters until pale and fluffy. Add the eggs one at a time, beating well after each addition. Sift the flour and baking powder over the mixture, then stir to combine. Spread the mixture evenly over the base of the prepared tin, then put the rhubarb over the top in a single layer. Sprinkle with the sugar. Bake for 40–45 minutes, or until golden. Leave to cool slightly in the tin, then carefully lift out, using the baking paper as handles, and cut into 5 cm (2 inch) squares. Dust with icing sugar and serve warm or at room temperature with whipped or thick cream.

Note: The rhubarb slice is best eaten on the day it is made.

Makes 24

In this Spanish-influenced recipe, sherry, orange and spices flavour a smoky-sweet sauce to complement baked apples.

baked apples with pedro ximénez sauce

3 tablespoons sultanas (golden raisins)
220 ml (7³/4 fl oz) Pedro Ximénez sherry (see Note)
butter, for greasing
1 teaspoon grated orange zest
2 tablespoons soft brown sugar
1/4 teaspoon ground cinnamon
50 g (1³/4 oz) butter, softened
30 g (1 oz/1/4 cup) toasted slivered almonds

6 small red apples (such as pink lady, gala or fuji), with stalks attached
6 whole cloves
110 g (3³/4 oz/scant ²/3 cup) raw caster (superfine) sugar
1 strip orange zest, no pith
1/2 cinnamon stick
vanilla ice cream or whipped cream, to serve

Put the sultanas in a small bowl with 1 tablespoon of the sherry and leave for 3–4 hours, or overnight.

Preheat the oven to 180°C (350°F/Gas 4) and liberally butter a shallow ovenproof dish. Mix the grated orange zest, brown sugar, cinnamon and half the butter together until smooth. Stir in the sultanas and almonds.

Cut the top one-quarter off each apple and stick a clove into the outside of each top. Cut out and discard the core, without cutting through the bottom of the apple. Fill the cavities with the sultana mixture and replace the apple tops. Put the apples in the prepared dish, sprinkle with 2 table-spoons of the raw caster sugar and put a little of the remaining butter on top of each apple. Pour water into the dish to a depth of 5 mm (^{1}/4 inch) and bake for 45–50 minutes, or until the apples are tender.

Put the remaining raw caster sugar, orange zest strip, cinnamon stick and 375 ml (13 fl oz/1^1/2 cups) water in a saucepan and stir over medium heat until the sugar dissolves. Bring to the boil, add the remaining sherry and return to the boil. Reduce the heat to low and simmer for 30–40 minutes, until it thickens to a glossy syrup. Strain into a small jug. Place the apples on serving plates, drizzle the warm syrup over them and serve with vanilla ice cream or whipped cream.

Note: Pedro Ximénez is a sherry made from the grape variety of the same name. Any other good-quality sweet dark sherry may be substituted.

Serves 6

baked apples with pedro ximénez sauce

pink grapefruit meringue tartlets

toffee-glazed poached pears with
caramel sauce

strawberry almond torte

crust
75 g (2 1/2 oz) butter, softened
40 g (1 1/2 oz) caster (superfine) sugar
1 teaspoon grated lemon zest
1/2 teaspoon natural vanilla extract
1 tablespoon strawberry liqueur
1 egg
1 egg yolk
75 g (2 1/2 oz/2/3 cup) ground almonds
1 1/2 tablespoons plain (all-purpose) flour

filling
250 g (9 oz) mascarpone cheese, softened
2 teaspoons icing (confectioners') sugar
35 g (1 1/4 oz) almond biscotti, crushed
1 teaspoon strawberry liqueur
1–2 tablespoons pouring (whipping) cream
500 g (1 lb 2 oz/3 1/3 cups) small strawberries, hulled
small mint leaves, to garnish (optional)
3 tablespoons strawberry jam, to glaze

Preheat the oven to 180°C (350°F/Gas 4) and grease a 23 cm (9 inch) springform cake tin. Beat the butter and sugar together until light and fluffy using electric beaters. Add the lemon zest, vanilla, strawberry liqueur, egg and egg yolk and mix until combined. Fold in the ground almonds and flour. Spoon the mixture into the prepared tin and level the top with the back of a spoon. Bake for 15–20 minutes, until set. Allow to cool in the tin for 5–10 minutes, then remove from the tin and transfer to a cake rack to cool completely.

For the filling, mix the mascarpone, icing sugar, crushed biscotti and strawberry liqueur together until smooth, then gently stir in enough cream to give a spreadable consistency. (The amount will depend on the thickness of the mascarpone.) Do not beat it in, as this may cause the mascarpone to split. Spread the mascarpone mixture over the top of the cake. Top with the strawberries. Scatter the mint leaves around, if using.

Put the jam in a small saucepan with 2 tablespoons water. Heat gently until the jam has melted, then strain it. Brush lightly over the strawberries and leave for the glaze to cool before serving.

Serves 6

strawberry almond torte

raspberry soufflé

crême pâtissière
3 egg yolks
60 g (2¼ oz/¼ cup) caster
(superfine) sugar
15 g (½ oz) cornflour
(cornstarch)
5 g (⅛ oz) plain (all-purpose)
flour
275 ml (9½ fl oz) milk
½ vanilla bean
10 g (¼ oz) butter
40 g (1½ oz) unsalted butter,
softened

185 g (6 oz) caster (superfine)
sugar

soufflé
400 g (14 oz/3¼ cups) fresh or
thawed frozen raspberries
3 tablespoons caster (superfine)
sugar
8 egg whites
icing (confectioners') sugar,
to dust

For the crême pâtissière, whisk together the egg yolks and half the sugar until pale and creamy. Sift in the cornflour and flour and mix together well. Put the milk, remaining sugar and vanilla bean in a saucepan. Bring just to the boil, then strain over the egg yolk mixture, stirring continuously. Pour back into a clean saucepan and bring to the boil, stirring constantly—it will be lumpy at first but will become smooth as you stir. Boil for 2 minutes, then stir in the 10 g (⅓ oz) butter and leave to cool. Transfer to a clean bowl, lay plastic wrap on the surface to prevent a skin forming and set aside until needed.

Brush the inside of a 1.5 litre (52 fl oz/6 cup) capacity soufflé dish with the softened butter. Pour in the caster sugar, turn the dish around to coat thoroughly and then tip out any excess sugar. Preheat the oven to 190°C (375°F/Gas 5) and put a baking tray in the oven to heat up.

For the soufflé, warm the crème pâtissière in a bowl over a saucepan of simmering water, then remove from the heat. Put the raspberries and half the sugar in a blender or food processor and mix until puréed (or mix by hand). Pass through a fine non-metallic sieve to get rid of the seeds. Add the crème pâtissière to the raspberries and whisk together.

Beat the egg whites in a clean, dry bowl until firm peaks form. Gradually whisk in the remaining sugar to make a stiff, glossy mixture. Whisk half the egg white into the raspberry mixture to loosen it and then fold in the remainder with a large metal spoon. Pour into the soufflé dish and run your thumb around the inside rim of the dish, about 2 cm (3/4 inch) into the soufflé mixture, to help the soufflé rise without sticking.

Put the dish on the hot baking tray and bake for 10–12 minutes, or until the soufflé is well risen and wobbles slightly when tapped. Test with a skewer through a crack in the side of the soufflé—the skewer should come out clean or very slightly moist. Serve immediately, dusted with a little icing sugar.

Serves 6

orange jelly and lime bavarois slice

orange jelly
1 tablespoon powdered gelatine
finely grated zest of 2 oranges
375 ml (13 fl oz/1^{1}/2 cups) fresh
    orange juice, strained
60 g (2^{1}/4 oz/^{1}/4 cup) caster
    (superfine) sugar
2 tablespoons Grand Marnier
    or other orange liqueur
    (optional)

lime bavarois
375 ml (13 fl oz/1^{1}/2 cups) milk
finely grated zest of 3 limes
4 egg yolks
120 g (4^{1}/4 oz/^{1}/2 cup) caster
    (superfine) sugar
125 ml (4 fl oz/^{1}/2 cup) fresh
    lime juice (about 5 limes)
3 teaspoons powdered gelatine
300 ml (10^{1}/2 fl oz) thickened
    (whipping) cream
8–10 small savoiardi (sponge
    finger) biscuits

Lightly grease an 11 x 22 cm (4^{1}/4 x 8^{1}/2 inch) loaf tin. Line across the tin and along its length with two sheets of baking paper that have been folded into triple thickness. Allow for plenty of overhang. Don't worry that the corners of the tin aren't lined; the paper is to give the bavarois a smooth surface and to enable it to be lifted out easily. Mix the gelatine with 2 tablespoons cold water in a small bowl. Put over a bowl of hot water and stir until dissolved.

For the orange jelly, put the zest, juice, sugar and liqueur in a saucepan and stir over low heat until the sugar dissolves. Simmer for 1 minute. Stir in the gelatine, then remove from the heat and cool to room temperature. Pour into the prepared tin and refrigerate for about 2 hours, or until set.

For the lime bavarois, heat the milk and zest in a saucepan until almost boiling. Beat the egg yolks and sugar with electric beaters until pale and creamy. Strain the hot milk in, beating continuously, then stir in the juice.

Mix the gelatine with 2 tablespoons cold water in a small bowl. Put over a bowl of hot water and stir until dissolved. Put the bowl containing the egg yolk and lime juice mixture over a saucepan of simmering water. Stir continuously for 15–20 minutes until the mixture thickens slightly. Stir the gelatine in, then remove from the heat and cool to room temperature. Whip the cream until soft peaks form, then gently fold it in to the gelatine mixture. Spoon this mixture over the set orange jelly. Arrange the savoiardi lengthways on top, covering the bavarois. Press them in gently. Refrigerate for 2–3 hours, or until firmly set.

To serve, invert onto a flat plate or board, then carefully peel the paper off. Serve cut into slices.

Serves 10

orange jelly and lime bavarois slice

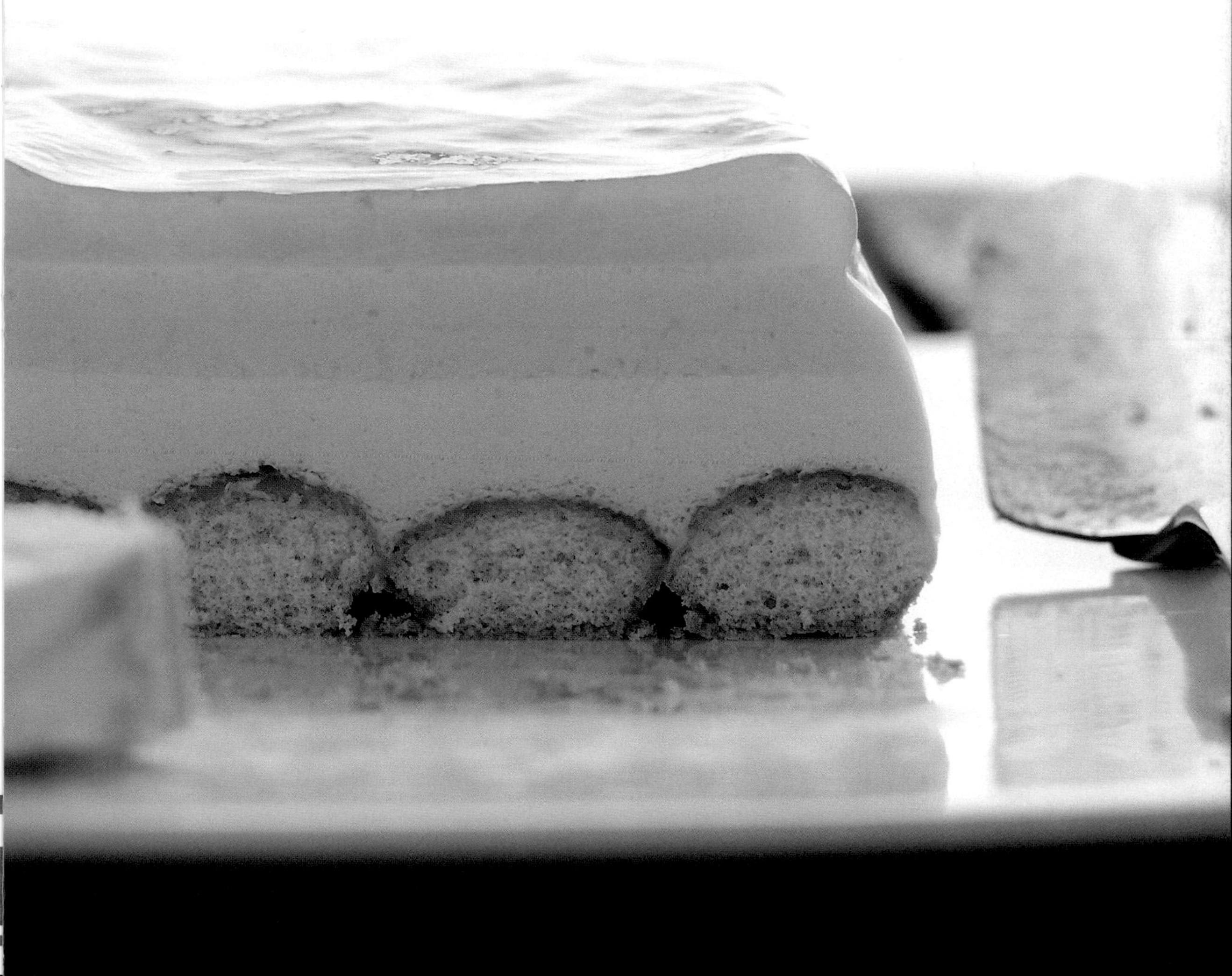

mixed berry sundae with
raspberry cream

Comforting yet refreshing at the same time, this pudding is very simple to make. Be sure to use the best ricotta you can find.

lime and ricotta pudding

60 g (2¼ oz/¼ cup) unsalted butter, softened

350 g (12 oz/1½ cups) caster (superfine) sugar

2 teaspoons finely grated lime zest

3 eggs, at room temperature, separated

375 g (13 oz/1½ cups) fresh ricotta cheese (see Note)

30 g (1 oz/¼ cup) self-raising flour

60 ml (2 fl oz/¼ cup) lime juice

2 teaspoons icing (confectioners') sugar

Preheat the oven to 180°C (350°F/Gas 4). Grease a 1.5 litre (52 fl oz/ 6 cup) capacity ovenproof dish.

Using electric beaters, beat the butter and caster sugar with half the lime zest for 30 seconds, or until combined. Add the egg yolks, one at a time, beating well after each addition. Gradually add the ricotta alternately with the flour and beat until thick and smooth. Stir in the lime juice.

Whisk the egg whites until stiff peaks form and gently fold into the ricotta mixture in two batches. Pour the mixture into the prepared dish and place in a roasting tin. Pour enough hot water into the tin to come halfway up the sides of the dish. Bake for 1 hour, or until the pudding is set.

Sift the icing sugar over the warm pudding and sprinkle with the remaining lime zest. Serve warm.

Note: The quality of the ricotta is important — it should be crumbly, moist and fresh tasting, not bland and dull. Buy bulk ricotta from a deli counter or specialist cheese store in preference to the prepackaged variety in tubs that is sold in supermarkets.

Serves 4

folded blueberry and raspberry tartlets

250 g (9 oz/2 cups) plain
   (all-purpose) flour
185 g (6$^1/_2$ oz/$^3/_4$ cup) cold
   butter, cubed
2 tablespoons caster (superfine)
   sugar

150 g (5$^1/_2$ oz/1 cup) fresh or
   frozen blueberries (see Note)
150 g (5$^1/_2$ oz/1$^1/_4$ cups) fresh or
   frozen raspberries (see Note)

40 g (1$^1/_2$ oz) caster (superfine)
   sugar
1 tablespoon plain (all-purpose)
   flour

1 egg, separated
4 sugar cubes, roughly crushed

thick (double/heavy) cream or
   ice cream, to serve

For the pastry, put the flour and butter in a food processor and process until fine and crumbly. Add the sugar and pulse briefly. Add 5 tablespoons cold water and pulse until the mixture just comes together. Turn out onto a flat surface and press into a smooth ball. Cover with plastic wrap and refrigerate for 30 minutes.

Preheat the oven to 210°C (415°F/Gas 6–7). Line a baking tray with baking paper.

Just before assembling the tart, put the fruit in a bowl and gently fold through the caster sugar and flour.

On a lightly floured surface, roll the pastry out to a thickness of about 3 mm (1/8 inch) and cut out four 16 cm (6 1/4 inch) rounds (you may need to cut two or three rounds and then reroll the pastry before cutting the rest). Transfer to the baking tray.

Brush the pastry with egg yolk thinned with 1 teaspoon water. Pile the combined fruit into the centre, leaving a 3 cm (1 1/4 inch) border. Fold and pleat the pastry edge to encase the fruit. Brush the edges with lightly beaten egg white and sprinkle over the crushed sugar cubes.

Bake for 15 minutes, reduce the oven to 200°C (400°F/Gas 6) and bake for about 25 minutes, or until the pastry is golden brown and crisp. Serve warm with thick cream or ice cream.

Note: If using frozen berries, spread them on a flat tray lined with paper towels and thaw in the refrigerator. Transfer them to the pastry with a slotted spoon to avoid excess liquid.

Makes 4

folded blueberry and raspberry tartlets

cardamom pear shortcake

250 g (9 oz) dried pears
1 tablespoon caster (superfine)
    sugar
275 g (9³/4 oz) unsalted butter,
    chopped
140 g (5 oz/³/4 cup lightly
    packed) soft brown sugar
80 g (2³/4 oz/¹/3 cup) caster
    (superfine) sugar

3 eggs
280 g (10 oz/2¹/4 cups) plain
    (all-purpose) flour
1 teaspoon baking powder
1 teaspoon ground cardamom
icing (confectioners') sugar,
    to dust

Put the dried pears in a bowl, cover with boiling water and soak for several hours, or until the pears have softened a little and the water has cooled.

Preheat the oven to 180°C (350°F/Gas 4). Lightly grease a 20 x 30 cm (8 x 12 inch) rectangular shallow tin with butter and line with baking paper, extending the paper to hang over the two long sides.

Drain the water from the pears, reserving 125 ml (4 fl oz/¹/2 cup). Put the pears, sugar and reserved soaking water in a saucepan. Stir to dissolve the sugar. Bring to the boil, then reduce the heat and simmer, covered, for 5 minutes, or until the pears are soft.

Cream the butter and sugars in a bowl using electric beaters until pale and fluffy. Add the eggs one at a time, beating well after each addition. Sift over the flour, baking powder and cardamom, then, using a large metal spoon, fold the flour mixture into the butter mixture until well combined. Spread half the mixture evenly over the base of the prepared tin. Arrange the pears over it, then dot the remaining mixture over the pears to cover.

Bake for 40–45 minutes, or until golden and a skewer inserted into the centre of the cake comes out clean. Leave to cool in the tin, then carefully lift out, using the baking paper as handles. Dust with icing sugar and cut into 10 x 3 cm (4 x 1 1/4 inch) fingers.

The cardamom pear shortcake will keep, stored in an airtight container in a cool place, for up to 3 days.

Makes 20

Can't decide between a fruit crumble and a tart? Try this recipe, a delicious melange of the two.

caramelized peach and passionfruit crumble tart

1 large sheet frozen ready-made shortcrust (pie) pastry (see Note)
80 g (2³/4 oz/²/3 cup) plain (all-purpose) flour
40 g (1¹/2 oz/¹/4 cup lightly packed) soft brown sugar
60 g (2¹/4 oz/¹/4 cup) unsalted butter, chilled and cubed
20 g (³/4 oz/¹/4 cup) desiccated (grated) coconut
2 tablespoons chopped roasted skinned hazelnuts (see Note, page 41)
4 peaches, peeled and sliced
80 g (2³/4 oz/¹/3 cup) caster (superfine) sugar
pulp of 3 passionfruit

Preheat the oven to 200°C (400°F/Gas 6). Roll out the pastry until large enough to cover the base and sides of a flan tin 20 cm (8 inches) across and 4 cm (1¹/2 inches) deep. Place the pastry in the tin and prick the base. Line the pastry shell with a sheet of baking paper and add baking beads or uncooked rice. Bake for 15 minutes, then remove the paper and weights and return to the oven for another 6–8 minutes. Remove from the oven and set aside to cool.

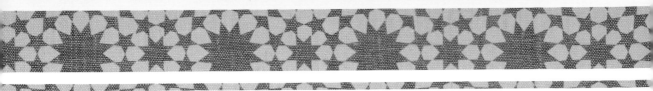

Reduce the oven to 180°C (350°F/Gas 4).

For the crumble, using your fingertips, rub the flour, brown sugar and butter together. Add the coconut and chopped hazelnuts. Set aside.

Heat a frying pan over high heat. Toss the peach slices in the caster sugar. Tip the peaches into the frying pan and cook, moving them occasionally, until they are evenly coated in caramel. Add the passionfruit pulp and remove the pan from the heat.

Spoon the peach mixture into the pastry case and top with the crumble mixture. Bake for 20–25 minutes, or until the top is golden brown.

Note: Choose a good-quality buttery pastry and let it sit for 20 minutes before rolling out, or it will crack and be difficult to work with.

Serves 6

caramelized peach and passionfruit
crumble tart

fig shortcake

185 g (6¹/₂ oz/1¹/₂ cups) plain
   (all-purpose) flour
60 g (2¹/₄ oz/¹/₂ cup) self-raising
   flour
2 teaspoons ground cinnamon
1 teaspoon ground ginger
1 teaspoon mixed (pumpkin pie)
   spice
115 g (4 oz/¹/₂ cup firmly
   packed) soft brown sugar
55 g (2 oz/¹/₂ cup) ground
   hazelnuts

125 g (4¹/₂ oz/¹/₂ cup) unsalted
   butter, chopped
1 egg, lightly beaten
315 g (11¹/₄ oz/1 cup) fig jam
95 g (3¹/₂ oz/²/₃ cup) hazelnuts,
   skinned, toasted and finely
   chopped (see Note, page 41)
icing (confectioners') sugar,
   to dust (optional)

whipped cream, to serve
   (optional)

Grease a 35 x 11 cm (14 x 4¹/₄ inch) loose-based rectangular tart tin.

Combine the flours, spices, sugar and hazelnuts in a food processor and process to just combine. Add the butter and, using the pulse button, process in short bursts until crumbly. Add the egg, a little at a time, until the mixture comes together; you may not need all the egg. Divide the dough in half, wrap each half separately in plastic wrap and refrigerate for 30 minutes.

Preheat the oven to 180°C (350°F/Gas 4).

Remove one ball of dough from the refrigerator and roll out between two sheets of baking paper until large enough to fit the base and sides of the tin. Line the prepared tin, gently pressing the pastry to fit into the corners, and patching any holes with extra dough. Trim away the excess.

Spread the pastry with the fig jam. Using the second chilled ball of dough, coarsely grate it into a bowl, add the chopped hazelnuts and gently toss to combine. Press the mixture gently over the top of the jam, taking care to retain the grated texture. Bake for 35 minutes, or until golden brown. Cool completely in the tin before cutting, and dust lightly with icing sugar to serve. Serve with whipped cream, if desired.

The shortcake will keep, stored in an airtight container, for up to 4 days, or up to 3 months in the freezer.

Serves 12

Cherries are at their prime in midsummer. Celebrate their brief but glorious season with this rustic open tart.

freeform apple and cherry tart

20 g (3/4 oz) butter
3 green apples, peeled, cored and cut into 1 cm (1/2 inch) pieces
60 g (21/4 oz/1/3 cup lightly packed) soft brown sugar
1/2 teaspoon ground cinnamon
1/2 teaspoon ground ginger
1/2 teaspoon lemon juice
2 tablespoons plain (all-purpose) flour

300 g (101/2 oz/11/2 cups) pitted fresh, thawed frozen or drained tinned cherries
1 large sheet pre-rolled, ready-made sweet shortcrust (pie) pastry
1 egg yolk
1 tablespoon milk
80 g (23/4 oz/1/4 cup) apricot jam

Preheat the oven to 180°C (350°F/Gas 4). Grease and flour a large baking tray or pizza tray.

Melt the butter in a saucepan over medium heat. Add the apples, brown sugar, spices and lemon juice and cook, covered, for 5 minutes, or until the apples have softened a little. Remove from the heat, cool a little, then stir in the flour and cherries. Allow to cool.

Trim the pastry to make a circle and place it onto the prepared tray. Pile the apple and cherry filling into the centre of the pastry, leaving a 5 cm (2 inch) border. Fold the pastry over the filling, leaving the centre uncovered, and pleating the pastry to fit. Combine the egg yolk and milk to make a glaze and brush it over the edges of the pastry. Bake the tart on the bottom shelf of the oven for 35–40 minutes, or until golden.

To make a jam glaze, combine the apricot jam and $1\frac{1}{2}$ tablespoons water in a small saucepan and bring to a simmer, stirring to combine. Brush the glaze over the pastry and fruit. Let the tart cool slightly before serving.

Serves 8

freeform apple and
cherry tart

banana fritters with butterscotch sauce

butterscotch sauce
60 g (2¹/₄ oz/¹/₄ cup) unsalted
    butter
115 g (4 oz/¹/₃ cup) golden syrup
    (light treacle) or dark corn
    syrup
60 g (2¹/₄ oz/¹/₃ cup lightly
    packed) soft brown sugar
55 g (2 oz/¹/₄ cup) caster
    (superfine) sugar
170 ml (5¹/₂ fl oz/²/₃ cup)
    pouring (whipping) cream
¹/₂ teaspoon natural vanilla
    extract

batter
125 g (4¹/₂ oz/1 cup) self-raising
    flour
1 egg, beaten, at room
    temperature
185 ml (6 fl oz/³/₄ cup) soda
    water
20 g (³/₄ oz) unsalted butter,
    melted

oil, for deep-frying
4 firm bananas
icing (confectioners') sugar, to
    dust (optional)
ice cream, to serve

For the butterscotch sauce, put the butter, golden syrup, brown sugar and caster sugar in a small saucepan. Stir over low heat for 2–3 minutes, or until the sugar has dissolved. Increase the heat and simmer for 3–5 minutes, taking care not to burn the sauce. Remove the pan from the heat and stir in the cream and vanilla.

For the batter, sift the flour into a bowl and make a well in the centre. Add the egg and soda water, whisk until smooth, then whisk in the butter.

Fill a saucepan one-third full of oil and heat to 200°C (400°F), or until a cube of bread dropped into the oil browns in 5 seconds.

Cut each banana lengthways into halves and add to the batter in batches. Use a spoon to coat the banana in the batter.

Using a slotted spoon, carefully lower the banana into the hot oil in batches. Fry each batch for 2–3 minutes, turning until the fritters are puffed and golden brown all over. Drain the fritters on paper towels. Serve the fritters hot, dusted with icing sugar, if desired. Accompany with ice cream and the butterscotch sauce.

Note: Any leftover sauce can be stored, covered, in the refrigerator for up to 2 weeks.

Serves 4

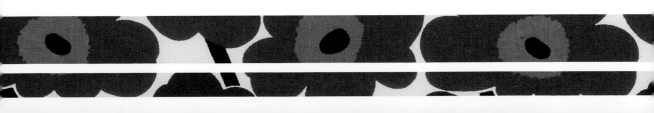

banana fritters with
butterscotch sauce

Most berries freeze wonderfully well, meaning that this luscious 'summer' pudding can be made all year round.

summer berry pudding

9 thin slices white bread, crusts removed (see Notes)

375 g (13 oz) mixed frozen berries (see Notes)

250 g (9 oz/2 cups) fresh or frozen raspberries (see Notes)

170 g–230 g (6–8^1/$_2$ oz/^{3}/$_4$–1 cup) caster (superfine) sugar, to taste

thick (double/heavy) cream or mascarpone cheese, to serve

Cut a circle from one of the slices of bread to fit the base of a 1 litre (35 fl oz/4 cup) capacity pudding basin. Cut the remaining bread slices into angled pieces and fit them around the basin, overlapping them as necessary. Reserve some bread for the top.

Put the berries in a large saucepan and gently stir in 170 g (6 oz/^{3}/$_4$ cup) of the sugar. Cover and simmer for 3–4 minutes, until the sugar has dissolved and the berry juices begin to run. Taste and check for sweetness, adding some of the remaining sugar if needed.

Strain 125 ml (4 fl oz/^{1}/$_2$ cup) of juice from the fruit and reserve. Spoon the fruit into the bread-lined basin using a slotted spoon. Pack it in well, then completely cover the top with the reserved bread slices. Put the pudding basin on a small baking tray. Cover the basin with plastic wrap and put a flat plate on top to fit neatly inside the rim. Put 2 heavy cans (or similar) on top to act as weights. Refrigerate overnight.

Just prior to serving, invert the pudding onto a serving plate. Spoon over the reserved juice to soak any bread that has not coloured. Cut into wedges and serve with thick cream or mascarpone.

Notes: For best results, use loaf bread thinly sliced rather than pre-sliced bread. The latter doesn't absorb juices as well as loaf bread. Put the frozen berries on a flat tray lined with paper towels and thaw in the refrigerator.

Serves 6–8

Calvados, a French apple brandy aged in oak, is the foundation of a rich sauce for these poached apples.

glazed apples with calvados sauce

230 g (8^1/$_2$ oz/1 cup) caster
   (superfine) sugar
1 strip lemon zest, no pith
1 tablespoon lemon juice
3 tablespoons Calvados
6 small to medium golden
   delicious apples

60 g (2^1/$_4$ oz/^{1}/$_4$ cup) butter,
   cubed
mascarpone cheese, to serve
4 small fresh lemon leaves
   (optional)

Put the sugar, lemon zest, lemon juice, half the Calvados and 650 ml (22^1/$_2$ fl oz) water into a saucepan large enough to take the apples in a single layer. Stir to dissolve the sugar, then bring to the boil.

Peel the apples, leaving the stalks intact. Add them to the syrup and poach over low heat until tender, 10–15 minutes, depending on the age of the apples. Carefully turn them once during cooking. Remove the apples once they are tender, put on serving plates and set aside until ready to serve.

Add the butter and lemon leaves, if using, to the pan, increase the heat and boil for 10–15 minutes, or until the syrup has thickened and darkened to a light caramel. Stir in the remaining Calvados.

Baste the apples with the syrup (use a bulb baster if you have one, as it makes it easier to draw up the syrup without damaging the apples) and discard the lemon zest. Serve hot or cold, with a dollop of mascarpone and the lemon leaves as garnish, if desired.

Serves 6

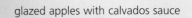

glazed apples with calvados sauce

summer berries in champagne jelly

1 litre (35 fl oz/4 cups)
    Champagne or sparkling
    white wine
1½ tablespoons powdered
    gelatine
250 g (9 oz) sugar

4 strips lemon zest
4 strips orange zest
250 g (9 oz/1²/₃ cups)
    strawberries, hulled
250 g (9 oz/1²/₃ cups)
    blueberries

Pour half the Champagne into a bowl and let the bubbles subside. Sprinkle the gelatine over the top in an even layer. Leave until the gelatine is spongy—do not stir. Pour the remaining Champagne into a large saucepan, add the sugar and zests and heat gently, stirring constantly, until all the sugar has dissolved. Remove the saucepan from the heat, add the gelatine mixture and stir until thoroughly dissolved. Leave to cool completely, then remove the zest.

Divide the berries among eight 125 ml (4 fl oz/½ cup) stemmed wine glasses and gently pour the jelly over them. Refrigerate until set. Remove from the refrigerator 15 minutes before serving.

Serves 8

cherry clafoutis

500 g (1 lb 2 oz) unpitted
   cherries, stems removed
60 g (2 1/4 oz/1/2 cup) plain
   (all-purpose) flour
90 g (3 1/4 oz/heaped 1/3 cup)
   caster (superfine) sugar
2 eggs, lightly beaten, at room
   temperature

200 ml (7 fl oz) milk
1 teaspoon natural vanilla
   extract
20 g (3/4 oz) unsalted butter,
   melted
icing (confectioners') sugar,
   to dust

Preheat the oven to 210°C (415°F/Gas 6–7). Lightly grease a 1.5 litre (52 fl oz/6 cup) capacity round ovenproof dish. Spread the cherries evenly over the base of the prepared dish.

Put the flour, sugar and a pinch of salt in a bowl and stir to combine. Add the eggs and beat well. Combine the milk, vanilla and butter, then pour into the egg mixture and beat until combined.

Carefully pour the batter over the cherries and bake for 40 minutes, or until the clafoutis is golden brown. Cool for at least 10 minutes, then serve warm or cold, dusted with icing sugar.

Serves 8

ricotta cake with fruits of the forest

cake
3 eggs
185 g (6^1/$_2$ oz) caster (superfine) sugar
125 g (4^1/$_2$ oz/1 cup) plain (all-purpose) flour
1 teaspoon baking powder
pinch of salt
1 tablespoon vegetable oil
100 ml (3^1/$_2$ fl oz) boiling water

filling
400 g (14 oz) ricotta cheese
200 g (7 oz) thick Greek-style yoghurt

150 g (5^1/$_2$ oz/1^1/$_4$ cups) icing (confectioners') sugar
350 ml (12 fl oz) thickened (whipping) cream
1 teaspoon natural vanilla extract

500 g (1 lb 2 oz) mixed fresh berries (see Notes)
2^1/$_2$ teaspoons powdered gelatine
2 teaspoons strawberry liqueur
100 g (3^1/$_2$ oz) caster (superfine) sugar
2 teaspoons lemon juice

For the cake, preheat the oven to 180°C (350°F/Gas 4). Grease a 25 cm (10 inch) round springform tin and line the base with baking paper.

Cream the eggs and sugar in a bowl for 3 minutes using electric beaters. Sift in the flour, baking powder and salt. Fold through. Add the oil and water and stir quickly until combined. Pour into the prepared tin and bake for 20 minutes, or until set. Turn out and cool completely on a wire rack.

For the filling, process the ricotta, yoghurt and icing sugar in a food processor until smooth. Whip the cream in a large bowl until stiff peaks form. Fold the ricotta through. Carefully fold in $1/2$ cup of the berries.

Using a long bread knife, carefully slice the cake in half horizontally. Put the bottom half back into the base of the cleaned reassembled springform tin. Spoon the ricotta mixture on top, then cover with the top of the cake. Press down firmly to eliminate air pockets. Put the tin on a large plate to collect any juices draining from the ricotta and refrigerate while you prepare the remaining berries.

Mix the gelatine and liqueur together in a small bowl and put over a bowl of hot water. Stir until dissolved. Put the remaining berries, the caster sugar and lemon juice in a pan and cook over high heat for 1–2 minutes, until the sugar dissolves and the mixture is syrupy but whole pieces of berry remain. Strain, reserving 125 ml (4 fl oz/$1/2$ cup) of syrup. Stir a spoonful or two of the reserved syrup into the gelatine mixture, then gently stir that back into the fruit. Cool for 10 minutes, then refrigerate for 30 minutes, until partially set. Spread the berry syrup over the cake leaving 1 cm ($1/2$ inch) around the edge uncovered. Refrigerate for 8 hours, or overnight, before serving.

Notes: Bulk ricotta from a deli counter is preferable to the pre-packed type in tubs. Use any seasonal berries; only use strawberries if they are very small.

Serves 8

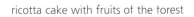
ricotta cake with fruits of the forest

blueberry semolina cakes

30 g (1 oz/^{1}/$_4$ cup) self-raising flour

40 g (1^1/$_2$ oz/^{1}/$_3$ cup) semolina

230 g (8 oz/1 cup) caster (superfine) sugar

25 g (1 oz/^{1}/$_4$ cup) ground almonds

^{1}/$_2$ teaspoon finely grated lemon zest

4 egg whites, lightly beaten

125 g (4^1/$_2$ oz/^{1}/$_2$ cup) unsalted butter, melted

80 g (2^3/$_4$ oz/^{1}/$_2$ cup) blueberries

45 g (1^1/$_2$ oz/^{1}/$_2$ cup) flaked almonds

icing (confectioners') sugar, to dust

Preheat the oven to 170°C (325°F/Gas 3). Line a 12-hole standard muffin tin with paper cases.

Sift the flour and semolina into a large bowl, add the sugar, ground almonds and lemon zest and stir to combine. Add the egg whites and, using electric beaters, beat until the ingredients are combined. Pour in the melted butter and continue to beat until smooth and well combined. Add the blueberries and fold in to just combine, then spoon the batter into the paper cases. Sprinkle the flaked almonds over the batter and bake for 30 minutes, or until a skewer inserted into the centre of a cake comes out clean. Turn out onto a wire rack to cool. Dust with icing sugar to serve. The blueberry cakes are best served on the day they are made.

Makes 12

peach galettes

1 quantity sweet shortcrust
   pastry (page 176)
600 g (1 lb 5 oz) peaches,
   stoned and thinly sliced
20 g (3/4 oz) butter, melted
1 tablespoon runny honey
1 tablespoon caster (superfine)
   sugar

1/4 teaspoon ground nutmeg
1 egg yolk
1 tablespoon milk
3 tablespoons apricot jam
25 g (1 oz/1/4 cup) flaked
   almonds, toasted

Lightly grease a baking tray or line it with baking paper. Roll out the pastry on a lightly floured work surface to 3 mm (1/8 inch) thick. Cut out twelve 12 cm (41/2 inch) rounds. Gently toss together the peach slices, butter, honey, sugar and nutmeg in a bowl. Divide the peach mixture among the pastry rounds, leaving a 1 cm (1/2 inch) border. Fold the pastry over the filling, leaving the centre uncovered, pleating the pastry at 1 cm (1/2 inch) intervals to fit. Place on the tray and refrigerate for 30 minutes.

Meanwhile, preheat the oven to 200°C (400°F/Gas 6). Combine the egg yolk and milk in a small bowl and brush this glaze over the edges of the pastry. Bake for 30 minutes, or until golden. In a small saucepan, stir the jam and 1 tablespoon water over low heat until smooth. Brush the mixture over the hot galettes, then sprinkle with almonds. Cool before serving.

Makes 12

citrus curd cake with kiwifruit

cake
185 g (6 1/2 oz/1 1/2 cups) self-
    raising flour
1 teaspoon baking powder
175 g (6 oz) butter, softened
175 g (6 oz/3/4 cup) caster
    (superfine) sugar
3 eggs
40 g (1 1/2 oz) desiccated
    (grated) coconut
finely grated zest of 1 lime
1 tablespoon lime juice
2 tablespoons milk

white chocolate cream
100 g (3 1/2 oz) white chocolate
250 ml (9 fl oz/1 cup) thickened
    (whipping) cream

citrus curd
3 tablespoons cornflour
4 tablespoons each lime, lemon
    and orange juice
185 g (6 1/2 oz) caster (superfine)
    sugar
3 egg yolks
20 g (3/4 oz) butter, softened

citrus syrup
125 g (4 1/2 oz) caster (superfine)
    sugar
1 tablespoon lime juice
1 tablespoon orange juice

4 ripe kiwifruit
35 g (1 1/4 oz/1/2 cup) flaked
    coconut, toasted

Preheat the oven to 180°C (350°F/Gas 4). Grease two 20 cm (8 inch) shallow sandwich tins and line the bases with baking paper. Sift the flour and baking powder into a bowl, add the butter, sugar, eggs, coconut, lime zest and juice and milk, and beat with electric beaters for 1 minute until smooth and creamy. Divide between the prepared tins and smooth the surface. Bake for 20–25 minutes, or until firm and springy to the touch. Remove from the oven, leave for 5 minutes, then turn out onto wire racks to cool completely. With a serrated knife, cut each cake in half horizontally.

For the white chocolate cream, put the chocolate in a heatproof bowl. Heat the cream in a small saucepan until hot. Pour the cream over the chocolate and stir until the chocolate has melted. Refrigerate until cold, then beat with electric beaters until soft peaks form.

For the citrus curd, put the cornflour, citrus juices, sugar, egg yolks and butter in a medium saucepan and whisk until smooth. Put over low heat and whisk until the mixture boils and thickens. Set aside to cool. For the citrus syrup, put the sugar, citrus juices and 3 tablespoons water in a small saucepan. Stir over medium heat to dissolve the sugar, then boil without stirring for 5 minutes, until a little syrupy. Brush all the cut surfaces of the cakes with the syrup. Peel and thinly slice the kiwifruit.

To assemble the cake, put one layer of cake on a serving plate. Spread with one-third of the citrus curd and arrange one-third of the kiwifruit slices on top. Continue this layering, ending with a cake layer on top. Spread the white chocolate cream all over the cake and scatter with toasted coconut.

Serves 10

alcoholic haze Normally when it comes to desserts, you think fruit, chocolate, cream, pastry — oh, and maybe a dash of alcohol would go nicely, too. This time it's the reverse: alcohol, in all its

myriad, heady, warming forms, is at the heart of these recipes. It's enough to make you pause for a fraction — just a fraction, mind — before turning the next page. Now, onwards and indulge!

What goes with alcohol? A lot, it would seem. Fruit of every season, from summery berries to winter's pears and blood oranges; nuts such as chestnuts and almonds; chocolate (of course); flavourings such as vanilla and coffee; and pastry and sweet breads such as madeira or pound cake and savoiardi (sponge finger) biscuits. You would be excused for thinking that just about any scrumptious dessert with a dash of alcohol could go in this chapter. Yet you would be wrong, for it is the alcohol that defines these recipes; without it, they just wouldn't be the same. A trifle is not a trifle without a splash of sherry or Marsala, and what to do with sober crepes? This is not a large chapter, which is perhaps a good thing, but each recipe is a pleasant voyage of discovery in the world of cooking with alcohol. Brandy, rum, whisky, red wine, cider, Kahlúa – all the old favourites are here, and a few more besides. With the well-chosen addition of alcohol, the flavour and aroma of a dish are unforgettably changed — desserts can become mellower and warmer, subtly sweet, or stronger and sharper. Many of the recipes in this chapter tread a simple path to your door, such as piña colada mousse or limoncello cream with tipsy ruby berries. There are, however, a few recipes that go for gold: Grand Marnier soufflés with liqueur sabayon spring to mind. In all cases, however, the presence of alcohol makes these dishes what they are — very nice, indeed.

285

apple cider dessert cake with cider sauce

cider sauce
1 litre (35 fl oz/4 cups) sweet
    alcoholic apple cider
60 ml (2 fl oz/1/4 cup) bourbon
3 tablespoons golden syrup (light
    treacle)
2 tablespoons cider vinegar
60 g (21/4 oz/1/3 cup lightly
    packed) dark brown sugar
1 cinnamon stick
1/2 teaspoon natural vanilla
    extract
250 ml (9 fl oz/1 cup) pouring
    (whipping) cream

cake
90 g (31/4 oz/1/3 cup) butter,
    softened
140 g (5 oz/3/4 cup lightly
    packed) dark brown sugar
1 teaspoon natural vanilla extract

2 eggs
210 ml (71/2 fl oz) sweet alcoholic
    apple cider
3 tablespoons vegetable oil
2 tablespoons bourbon
225 g (8 oz/heaped 13/4 cups)
    plain (all-purpose) flour
1 teaspoon baking powder
1/4 teaspoon bicarbonate of soda
    (baking soda)
1 teaspoon salt

topping
185 ml (6 fl oz/3/4 cup) thickened
    (whipping) cream
3 tablespoons thick Greek-style
    yoghurt
1/4 teaspoon natural vanilla
    extract
1 teaspoon caster (superfine)
    sugar

For the sauce, put the cider, bourbon, golden syrup, vinegar, sugar and
cinnamon stick in a large saucepan and bring to the boil. Simmer over low
heat for 10 minutes, then stir in the vanilla and cream. Increase the heat

to medium and boil for 40 minutes, or until reduced to about 250 ml (9 fl oz/1 cup); do not let it burn. Discard the cinnamon stick.

For the cake, preheat the oven to 180°C (350°F/Gas 4). Grease a 20 cm (8 inch) springform cake tin and line the bottom with baking paper. Flour the sides of the tin. In a large bowl, beat the butter until creamy using electric beaters. Add the sugar and vanilla and beat until smooth. Add the eggs one at a time, beating well after each addition.

Mix the cider, oil and bourbon in a jug. Sift the flour, baking powder, bicarbonate of soda and salt into a bowl. Fold into the butter mixture in three batches, alternating with the cider mixture. Spoon two-thirds of the batter into the prepared tin. Using a spoon, carefully drizzle half of the cider sauce over the top. Gently spoon the remaining batter on top and spread it evenly, being careful not to mix the layers. Bake for 45 minutes, or until a skewer inserted in the centre comes out clean. Cool in the tin for 10 minutes, then turn out onto a wire rack. Cool for 15 minutes, then peel off the baking paper. Cool for a further 15 minutes.

For the topping, whip the cream, yoghurt and vanilla until soft peaks form. Gradually incorporate the caster sugar and continue whipping until stiff. Spread the topping over the top of the cake and level the surface.

Reheat the remaining cider sauce. Slice the cake into wedges and serve warm or cold, with a little warm cider sauce drizzled over the top.

Serves 8

trifle

hot chocolate soufflé with brandy chocolate sauce

chocolate brandy sauce
90 g (3¼ oz) dark chocolate, chopped
30 g (1 oz) butter, cubed
125 ml (4 fl oz/½ cup) pouring (whipping) cream
2 tablespoons icing (confectioners') sugar
2 tablespoons brandy

caster (superfine) sugar, to sprinkle

soufflé
125 g (4½ oz/heaped ¾ cup) chopped dark chocolate
4 eggs, separated
1 teaspoon natural vanilla extract
2 egg whites, extra

icing (confectioners') sugar, to dust
pouring (whipping) cream, to serve

For the chocolate brandy sauce, heat the chocolate and butter in a heatproof bowl over (not touching) a saucepan of simmering water, stirring often, until just melted and smooth. Whisk in the cream, icing sugar and brandy. Set aside.

Preheat the oven to 200°C (400°F/Gas 6). Butter a 1.25 litre (44 fl oz/ 5 cup) soufflé dish and sprinkle with caster sugar. Tap out the excess. Fix a collar around the dish (see Note).

For the soufflé, heat the chocolate in a heatproof bowl over (not touching) a saucepan of simmering water, stirring often, until just melted. Remove from the heat and whisk in the egg yolks and vanilla.

Put the six egg whites in a clean bowl. Beat with electric beaters until firm peaks form. Stir one-quarter of the egg white into the chocolate mixture with a large metal spoon, then gently fold in the remainder. Pour into the prepared dish. Put the dish on a baking tray and bake for 20–25 minutes, or until puffed and firm to the touch.

Gently reheat the chocolate sauce and pour it into a small jug.

Dust the soufflé with icing sugar and serve at once, accompanied by the sauce and pouring cream.

Note: For the collar, cut a sheet of baking paper long enough to wrap around the dish and fold it into thirds lengthways. Grease the inner surface lightly. Wrap it around the dish so that it stands 3–4 cm (about 1 1/2 inches) higher than the rim of the dish, and tie in position with jute or cotton string.

Serves 4

crepes with passionfruit liqueur butter

crepes
125 g (4¹/₂ oz/1 cup) plain
   (all-purpose) flour
2 eggs, lightly beaten
300 ml (10¹/₂ fl oz) milk
30 g (1 oz) butter, melted
1 teaspoon grated lime zest
1 tablespoon Galliano liqueur

passionfruit liqueur butter
115 g (4 oz/¹/₂ cup) caster
   (superfine) sugar
125 ml (4 fl oz/¹/₂ cup) strained
   passionfruit juice (see Note)
1 teaspoon grated lime zest
3 tablespoons Galliano liqueur

30 g (1 oz) butter, cubed
ice cream or pouring (whipping)
   cream, to serve

Put the flour in a food processor and briefly process. With the motor running, pour in the eggs and one-quarter of the milk. Process until incorporated. Add the remaining milk, melted butter, lime zest and liqueur. Process until smooth. Pour into a jug and set aside for 20 minutes.

Heat a lightly greased 17 cm (6¹/₂ inch) crepe pan. Pour in a thin layer of batter to cover the pan completely and tip out any excess. Cook over medium heat until lightly golden and crisp around the edges, then turn and cook the other side. Transfer to a side plate. Cook the remaining

batter, stacking the crepes. You will need 12 crepes, so there is enough batter for a couple of failures.

For the passionfruit butter, put the sugar and 3 tablespoons water in a large frying pan. Stir over medium heat to dissolve the sugar. Increase the heat and boil without stirring for 3–4 minutes until the sugar has evenly caramelized to a rich dark colour. Lower the heat, then carefully and slowly pour on the passionfruit juice, taking care as it will spit. Cook, stirring, over low heat until the caramel has dissolved. Stir in the grated lime zest and liqueur.

Fold each of the 12 crepes into quarters and arrange them overlapping in the sauce. Dot with the diced butter. Over a low heat, gently shake the pan and spoon the sauce over the crepes until the butter melts and mixes into the sauce. Serve three per person, with ice cream or pouring cream.

Note: You will need the pulp of about 9 passionfruit, sieved, to yield 125 ml (4 fl oz/1/2 cup) of juice.

Serves 4

crepes with passionfruit liqueur butter

chocolate rum mousse

250 g (9 oz/1²/₃ cups) chopped
    dark chocolate
3 eggs
60 g (2¹/₄ oz/¹/₄ cup) caster
    (superfine) sugar

2 teaspoons dark rum
250 ml (9 fl oz/1 cup) thickened
    (whipping) cream, softly
    whipped

Heat the chocolate in a heatproof bowl over (not touching) a saucepoan of simmering water, stirring occasionally, until melted. Set aside to cool.

Beat the eggs and sugar in a small bowl using electric beaters for 5 minutes, or until thick, pale and increased in volume. Transfer the mixture to a large bowl. Using a metal spoon, fold in the melted chocolate with the rum. Leave to cool, then fold in the whipped cream until just combined.

Spoon into four 250 ml (9 fl oz/1 cup) ramekins or dessert glasses. Refrigerate for 2 hours, or until set.

Serves 4

zuppa inglese

4 thick slices sponge or
    Madeira (pound) cake
80 ml (2¹/2 fl oz/¹/3 cup) kirsch
150 g (5¹/2 oz/1¹/4 cups)
    raspberries
170 g (6 oz/1¹/3 cups)
    blackberries
2 tablespoons caster
    (superfine) sugar

250 ml (9 fl oz/1 cup) vanilla
    custard (homemade or
    purchased)
250 ml (9 fl oz/1 cup) thickened
    (whipping) cream, lightly
    whipped
icing (confectioners') sugar,
    to dust

Put a piece of sponge cake on each of four deep plates and brush or
sprinkle it with the kirsch. Leave the kirsch to soak in for a minute or two.

Put the raspberries and blackberries in a saucepan with the caster sugar.
Gently warm through over low heat so that the sugar just melts, then
leave the fruit to cool.

Spoon the fruit over the sponge, pour the custard on top of the berries,
dollop the cream on top and dust with icing sugar. Serve immediately.

Serves 4

vanilla bean liqueur panna cotta with liqueur berries

435 ml (15¼ fl oz/1¾ cups) pouring (whipping) cream

3 tablespoons caster (superfine) sugar

½ vanilla bean, split

2 teaspoons powdered gelatine

2 tablespoons Drambuie (or similar) liqueur (see Note)

300 g (10½ oz) mixed fresh or thawed frozen berries (see Notes)

3 tablespoons icing (confectioners') sugar

3 tablespoons Drambuie

Put the cream, sugar and vanilla bean in a saucepan and stir to dissolve the sugar. Bring slowly just to the boil, then remove from the heat. Set aside for 5 minutes to cool a little.

Scrape the seeds from the vanilla bean into the mixture and discard the pod. Put the gelatine and 1 tablespoon cold water in a small bowl. Set over another bowl of hot water to dissolve the gelatine. Stir the dissolved gelatine into the cream mixture and then stir in the liqueur. Strain the

mixture into a jug then divide among four 125 ml (4 fl oz/$1/2$ cup) dariole, metal or ceramic moulds. Cover with plastic wrap, put on a tray and refrigerate at least 4 hours, or overnight, until set.

Meanwhile, combine the berries, icing sugar and Drambuie. Set aside for at least 1 hour, so the berries can absorb the flavours and become juicy.

To unmould the panna cottas, briefly dip the moulds into hot water and loosen the edges with a small knife. Turn out onto serving plates. Serve with the berries and drizzle over some of the juice.

Notes: Drambuie is a Scotch-whisky-based liqueur sweetened with honey and flavoured with herbs. If using frozen berries, put them in a single layer on a metal tray lined with paper towels and thaw in the refrigerator.

Serves 4

vanilla bean liqueur panna cotta
with liqueur berries

piña colada mousse

2 scant teaspoons powdered
  gelatine
4 tablespoons piña colada (see
  Notes)
50 g (1³/4 oz) butter
1/2 teaspoon natural vanilla
  extract
150 g (5¹/2 oz/1 cup) finely
  chopped white chocolate
3 eggs, separated
1 egg white

2 tablespoons caster (superfine)
  sugar
125 ml (4 fl oz/¹/2 cup)
  thickened (whipping) cream,
  whipped
1/2 fresh coconut, to garnish
  (optional)
3 thin slices fresh pineapple,
  to garnish
2 tablespoons fresh passionfruit
  pulp, to garnish

Mix the gelatine and half the piña colada in a small bowl. Put over a bowl of hot water and stir until dissolved. Melt the butter, vanilla and remaining piña colada in a small saucepan over low heat. Remove from the heat and add the chocolate. Stir until the chocolate has melted and the mixture is smooth. Stir in the gelatine. Transfer to a bowl and add the egg yolks one at a time, beating well after each addition. Allow to cool.

Whisk the four egg whites until soft peaks form. Gradually add the sugar and continue whisking until firm peaks form. Using a metal spoon, fold a heaped spoonful of the whites into the chocolate mixture to loosen it, then gently fold in the remainder.

Carefully fold in the whipped cream. Spoon the mixture into six individual glass bowls, cover with plastic wrap and refrigerate overnight.

If garnishing with the coconut, preheat the grill (broiler) to medium. Using a vegetable peeler, cut thin curling lengths from the outer edges of the coconut, including the brown skin. Spread on a baking sheet and grill (broil) for 2–3 minutes, or until crisp and lightly coloured (see Notes).

Using a sharp knife, quarter the pineapple slices and cut out the core.

Top each glass of mousse with one or two coconut twists and a couple of pineapple pieces stuck in at a jaunty angle. Drizzle just a little passionfruit over the pineapple to serve.

Notes: Instead of the piña colada, you can use 2 tablespoons each of pineapple juice and Malibu (coconut and rum liqueur). Unused coconut curls can be kept in an airtight container for many weeks, then re-crisped in the oven.

Serves 6

grand marnier soufflés with liqueur sabayon

caster (superfine) sugar, to
  sprinkle

60 g (2¼ oz/¼ cup) butter,
  chopped
80 g (2¾ oz/⅓ cup) caster
  (superfine) sugar
1 tablespoon grated orange zest
2 tablespoons plain (all-purpose)
  flour
1 tablespoon cornflour
  (cornstarch)
3 tablespoons Grand Marnier
  or other orange liqueur
250 ml (9 fl oz/1 cup) milk

4 eggs, separated
2 egg whites

liqueur sabayon
2 egg yolks
80 g (2½ oz/⅓ cup) caster
  (superfine) sugar
80 ml (2¾ fl oz/⅓ cup)
  Sauternes, white wine
  or sweet sherry
1 tablespoon Grand Marnier or
  other orange liqueuer

icing (confectioners') sugar, to
  dust

Preheat the oven to 200°C (400°F/Gas 6). Grease six 250 ml (9 fl oz/1 cup) soufflé dishes and sprinkle the sides and base with caster sugar, tapping out the excess. Put the dishes on a baking tray.

Put the butter, sugar and zest in a small bowl and beat with electric beaters for 2 minutes until creamy. Beat in the flour, cornflour and liqueur.

Meanwhile, bring the milk to the boil in a medium saucepan. With beaters running, slowly pour the hot milk into the butter and flour mixture, beating constantly until smooth. Return the mixture to the saucepan and beat constantly over the heat until it boils and thickens. Beat in the egg yolks. Transfer to a large bowl.

Whisk the six egg whites in a large, clean bowl until soft peaks form. Use a metal spoon to stir one-third of the egg white into the flour mixture, then carefully fold in the remaining white. Spoon into the prepared dishes. Bake for 15–18 minutes until well risen and cooked.

Meanwhile, make the liqueur sabayon. Put the egg yolks and sugar in a bowl and beat with electric beaters until creamy. Immerse the bowl in a large pan of simmering water and continue to beat for a further 1 minute (take care that the cord of the beaters is kept well away from the heat).

Pour in the wine or sherry and Grand Marnier. Beat for 5–7 minutes until tripled in volume and mousse-like. Remove from the heat and continue to beat for 1 minute. Pour into a serving jug.

Serve the soufflés immediately, dusted lightly with icing sugar and with some sabayon poured over the top.

Serve 6

grand marnier soufflés with
liqueur sabayon

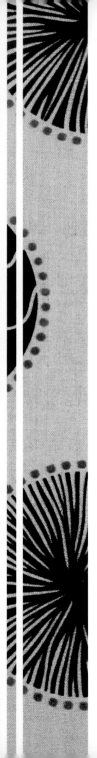

amaretti apple stack with caramel sauce

125 g (4¹/2 oz/1 cup) plain
    (all-purpose) flour
2 eggs
250 ml (9 fl oz/1 cup) milk
30 g (1 oz) unsalted butter,
    melted
1 tablespoon Amaretto liqueur
    (optional)
extra butter, for frying

125 g (4¹/2 oz) amaretti biscuits
5 cooking apples, peeled, cored
    and very thinly sliced

185 g (6¹/2 oz/³/4 cup) unsalted
    butter
185 g (6¹/2 oz/1 cup lightly
    packed) light brown sugar
175 g (6 oz/¹/2 cup) golden syrup
    (light treacle)
125 ml (4 fl oz/¹/2 cup) pouring
    (whipping) cream
185 g (6¹/2 oz/³/4 cup) light sour
    cream

Sift the flour into a large bowl and make a well in the centre. Gradually whisk in the combined eggs and milk until the batter is smooth and free of lumps. Mix in the butter and Amaretto. Transfer to a jug, cover and leave for 30 minutes to thicken.

Heat a small crepe pan or non-stick frying pan and brush lightly with melted butter. Pour a little batter into the pan, swirling quickly, to thinly cover the base, pouring any excess back into the jug. Cook for 30 seconds, or until the edges just begin to curl, then turn and cook the other side until lightly browned. Transfer to a plate and cover with a clean cloth.

Repeat with the remaining batter to make 10 crepes, greasing the pan when necessary. Stack the crepes between baking paper to prevent them from sticking together.

Preheat the oven to 180°C (350°F/Gas 4). Roughly chop the amaretti in a food processor. Place on a baking tray and bake for 5–8 minutes, stirring occasionally, until crisp.

Mix the apple slices in a bowl with 60 g (2¼ oz/¼ cup) of the butter, melted, and half the brown sugar. Spread evenly onto a tray and place under a moderate grill (broiler) for 5 minutes. Turn and grill (broil) until light brown and soft (you may need to do this in batches). Set aside.

Put a crepe on a large heatproof plate. Spread evenly with some apple, slightly mounded in the middle, and sprinkle with chopped amaretti. Continue to fill and layer in this manner until all the crepes are stacked. Cover with foil and heat in the oven for 10 minutes, or until warm.

Put the remaining brown sugar, golden syrup, cream and remaining butter in a small pan. Stir over low heat until the sugar has dissolved, then simmer for 1 minute. Spread the top crepe with sour cream. Pour a little warm sauce over the pancake stack and cut into wedges to serve.

Serves 4–6

The sweet warmth of Cointreau gives bite to this simple upside-down dessert of pastry circles topped with orange slices.

orange galette with cointreau

2 pre-rolled sheets puff pastry
50 g (1¾ oz) butter, softened
50 g (1¾ oz/¼ cup firmly
    packed) dark brown sugar
3 small oranges

2 teaspoons raw caster
    (superfine) sugar
2 teaspoons Cointreau or other
    orange liqueur
whipped cream, to serve

Cut a 24 cm (9½ inch) round from each of the pastry sheets. Put them on a baking tray, prick all over with a fork and refrigerate until needed.

Grease two 24 cm (9½ inch) metal pie dishes (measured across the top). Cream the butter and dark brown sugar until the sugar dissolves. Divide the mixture between the prepared dishes and spread it evenly over the bases. Chill while preparing the oranges.

Preheat the oven to 190°C (375°F/Gas 5). Using a vegetable peeler, remove and discard the zest from the oranges, leaving a good amount of pith on the orange. Cut the oranges into thin, even slices, discarding any seeds.

Don't use a serrated knife, as it will tear the flesh. Get rid of the juice by gently squeezing a stack of slices between your hands into the sink to remove as much juice as possible.

Arrange the slices, slightly overlapping, over the tart bases. Scatter the caster sugar over then sprinkle the Cointreau on top. Cover with the pastry rounds, pricked side up.

Bake on separate racks in the oven for 15 minutes, then swap them over and bake for 20–25 minutes, or until the pastry is crisp and golden. Don't worry if the pastry shrinks.

Remove the tarts from the oven, wait for 30–40 seconds, then quickly invert them onto flat plates. Put one on top of the other, with the oranges uppermost. Leave to settle for a minute, then serve immediately, with whipped cream.

Serves 6–8

orange galette with cointreau

limoncello cream with tipsy ruby berries

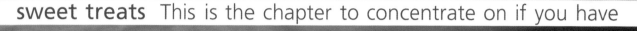

sweet treats This is the chapter to concentrate on if you have children. If not, borrow some. Any collection of bumpy, crunchy, crackly, nutty concoctions like these is not meant to be taken too

seriously. On the other hand … we all need to look after the child within every now and then, and rum truffles really are a mature taste. So free your inner child and go wild with sweet treats.

This chapter starts with a bang: honeycomb. If you didn't know it before, you soon will: honeycomb is really, terribly, wonderfully bad for you. The first three ingredients are essentially sugar: caster (superfine) sugar, honey and liquid glucose. Then, 1 tablespoon of bicarbonate of soda (baking soda) later and its back to the sweet stuff, with a good helping of dark chocolate. And that's it. Well, so much for the first recipe, which fairly accurately sets the tone for what's to come. That is, an indulgent chapter of biscuits, crisp wafers and what can only be described as gooey, chocolatey, crunchy-munchy things. Sugar, in all its glorious forms, appears with cheerful regularity, but also playing their part in this conspiracy to tempt us away from the straight and narrow are chocolate, cream, dried fruit, nuts and alcohol. There is something for everyone here, from child-friendly snack food to sophisticated finishing touches for a dinner party. There are classic accompaniments to tea and coffee, such as Florentines and creamy coconut ice. As well, quite a number of recipes that we probably shouldn't make, let alone eat, are also included, chief among them rocky road, but we should hasten to add that you're not meant to eat the whole thing in one sitting. White chocolate bark just begs to be investigated, whereas no-bake chocolate squares — well, obviously, you're making them for the kids. At heart, these are recipes for putting aside caution and just enjoying a mouthful or two of a little sweet something.

honey and nut chocolate wafers

chocolate, nut and ginger pâté

250 g (9 oz/1²/₃ cups) chopped
dark chocolate

20 g (³/₄ oz) butter

160 ml (5¹/₄ fl oz) sweetened
condensed milk

2 tablespoons rum or brandy

70 g (2¹/₂ oz/¹/₂ cup) hazelnuts,
roasted and skinned (see
Note, page 41)

80 g (2³/₄ oz/¹/₂ cup) roasted,
unsalted macadamia nuts

50 g (1³/₄ oz/¹/₃ cup) whole
almonds, roasted

70 g (2¹/₂ oz/¹/₃ cup) glacé
(candied) ginger, finely
chopped

Grease a 25 x 8 cm (10 x 3¹/₄ inch) loaf (bar) tin and line it with baking paper. Extend the paper over the long sides for easy removal later.

Heat the chocolate in a heatproof bowl over (not touching) a saucepan of gently simmering water, stirring frequently, until just melted and smooth. Add the butter, condensed milk and rum or brandy. Stir until smooth. Remove from the heat, add the nuts and ginger and mix thoroughly. Spoon into the prepared tin and smooth the surface. Cover and refrigerate for several hours until firm. Serve chilled, cut into wafer-thin slices, with coffee. Store in the refrigerator for up to 3 weeks.

Makes about 50 slices

peanut chews

70 g (2¹/₂ oz/scant ¹/₂ cup)
   roasted unsalted peanuts
250 g (9 oz) sugar
250 ml (9 fl oz/1 cup) pouring
   (whipping) cream

30 g (1 oz) butter
2 tablespoons clear honey
2–3 drops natural vanilla extract

Line a 20 cm (8 inch) square slice tin with a double thickness of baking paper. Extend the paper over two sides for easy removal later. Scatter the peanuts over the base. Put the sugar, cream, butter, honey and vanilla into a heavy-based saucepan and stir over low heat until the sugar has dissolved. Using a pastry brush dipped in cold water, brush down the sides of the pan to remove any sugar crystals. Bring to the boil and boil over a medium–low heat, stirring occasionally, until deep golden in colour and a few drops form a semi-soft ball when dropped into a bowl of cold water (120°C (235°F) on a sweets (candy) thermometer). This will be the consistency of the finished chews, so cook the mixture for a little longer if it feels too soft.

Immediately pour the mixture over the peanuts in the prepared tin. Level the surface and leave for about 2 hours to cool. Lift out, using the paper as handles, and cut into logs using a buttered knife. Wrap the logs in cellophane, bonbon style, to prevent them from sticking together.

Makes about 40

rum and raisin bagatelles

100 g (3^1/$_2$ oz/heaped ^{3}/$_4$ cup)
   raisins
1 tablespoon Malibu (coconut
   and rum liqueur)
50 g (1^3/$_4$ oz/^{3}/$_4$ cup) shredded
   coconut

400 g (14 oz/2^2/$_3$ cups) chopped
   dark chocolate
100 g (3^1/$_2$ oz/^{2}/$_3$ cup) pine nuts,
   toasted

Put the raisins and Malibu in a small bowl, cover and leave overnight.

Preheat the oven to 150°C (300°F/Gas 2). Spread the coconut on a baking tray and bake for 5–10 minutes, or until lightly golden. Remove from the oven, lift the baking paper and coconut off the tray and put to one side to cool. Line the baking tray with fresh baking paper. Heat the chocolate in a heatproof bowl over (not touching) a saucepan of gently simmering water, stirring frequently, until melted and smooth. Drain the raisins well. Remove the chocolate from the heat and stir in the raisins, coconut and pine nuts. Using oiled teaspoons, take spoonfuls of mixture and shape into loose balls. Don't squash them too firmly, but just enough for them to cling together, with bits of coconut and pine nuts sticking out. Put onto the prepared tray. Leave to dry, then refrigerate until set completely. Store in an airtight container in the refrigerator for up to 2 weeks.

Makes about 32

white chocolate bark

150 g (5^1/$_2$ oz/1 cup) roasted
   unsalted macadamia nuts,
   chopped
250 g (9 oz/1^2/$_3$ cups) chopped
   white chocolate

120 g (4^1/$_4$ oz/^{2}/$_3$ cup) dried
   apricots, finely chopped
50 g (1^3/$_4$ oz/^{1}/$_3$ cup) currants

Preheat the oven to 180°C (350°F/Gas 4) and line a baking tray with baking paper. Spread the nuts over a second baking tray. Roast until lightly browned, 5–6 minutes, shaking the tray once or twice to ensure even roasting. Cool.

Heat the chocolate in a heatproof bowl over (not touching) a saucepan of simmering water until just melted and smooth. Remove from the heat. Add two-thirds of the nuts and dried fruit and stir to coat.

Pour the mixture into the prepared tray and spread to a square of approximately 25 cm (10 inches). Scatter over the remaining nuts and fruit. Cover with plastic wrap and refrigerate until set. Break into large chunks and store in an airtight container in the refrigerator. It will keep for 3 weeks.

Serves 8–10

white chocolate bark

no-bake chocolate squares

100 g (3^1/$_2$ oz) shortbread
biscuits, roughly crushed
120 g (4^1/$_4$ oz) pistachio nuts
150 g (5^1/$_2$ oz/1 cup) hazelnuts,
toasted and skinned
100 g (3^1/$_2$ oz/^{1}/$_2$ cup) glacé
(candied) cherries, roughly
chopped

300 g (10^1/$_2$ oz/2 cups) chopped
good-quality dark chocolate
200 g (7 oz) unsalted butter,
chopped
1 teaspoon instant coffee
granules
2 eggs, lightly beaten

Lightly grease an 18 x 27 cm (7 x 10^3/$_4$ inch) baking tin and line with baking paper, extending the paper over the two long sides for easy removal later. Combine the biscuits, pistachios, 90 g (3^1/$_4$ oz/^{2}/$_3$ cup) of the hazelnuts, and half the cherries.

Heat the chocolate and butter in a heatproof bowl over (not touching) a saucepan of simmering water, stirring occasionally, until melted and smooth. Remove from the heat and when the mixture has cooled slightly, mix in the coffee and eggs. Pour over the nut mixture and mix well. Pour the mixture into the tin and pat down well. Roughly chop the remaining hazelnuts and sprinkle them over the top with the remaining cherries. Refrigerate overnight. Remove from the tin and trim the edges of the slice before cutting into pieces. Store in an airtight container in the refrigerator.

Makes 18

almond fruit bread

3 egg whites

125 g (4 1/2 oz) caster (superfine) sugar

125 g (4 1/2 oz/1 cup) plain (all-purpose) flour, sifted

125 g (4 1/2 oz) unblanched almonds

100 g (3 1/2 oz/1/2 cup) glacé (candied) cherries

30 g (1 oz) glacé (candied) apricots, cut into pieces the same size as the cherries

30 g (1 oz) glacé (candied) pineapple, cut into pieces the same size as the almonds

Preheat the oven to 180°C (350°F/Gas 4). Grease a 25 x 8 cm (10 x 3 1/4 inch) bar tin and line it with baking paper. Whisk the egg whites in a bowl until soft peaks form, then gradually add the sugar, whisking continuously, and continue whisking until very stiff peaks form. Fold through the flour. Gently fold in the almonds and dried fruits. Smooth the surface and bake for 30–40 minutes, until firm to the touch. Cool in the tin for 10 minutes, then turn out and peel off the baking paper. Cool completely on a wire rack, then wrap in foil and set aside for 1–2 days.

Preheat the oven to 140°C (275°F/Gas 1) and line a baking tray with baking paper. Using a very sharp knife, cut the loaf into wafer-thin slices. Spread on the baking tray and bake for 45–50 minutes until dry and crisp. Cool on the tray before storing in an airtight container.

Makes 30–40 slices

Praline — a mixture of nuts and toffee — gives a delicate crunch to these rich morsels.

praline liqueur-filled chocolate dates

praline filling
50 g (1 3/4 oz/1/3 cup) chopped
  dark chocolate
30 g (1 oz) butter, softened
2 tablespoons vienna almonds,
  chopped medium-fine
  (see Notes)

1 tablespoon Grand Marnier or
  other orange liqueur
15 fresh dates (see Notes)

50 g (1 3/4 oz/1/3 cup) chopped
  milk chocolate

For the praline filling, put the chocolate in a heatproof bowl over (not touching) a saucepan of simmering water and stir until just melted and smooth. Remove from the heat and set aside to cool.

In a small bowl, whisk the butter until pale and creamy. Whisk in the melted chocolate, then add the ground almonds and Grand Marnier. Cover and refrigerate until firm but not hard.

Use a small sharp knife to make a slit along each date and remove the stone. Put the praline filling in a small sturdy plastic bag and snip off a corner. Use as a piping bag to fill the dates with the filling. Smooth off the filling along the cut edge with a small knife. Refrigerate on a tray.

Heat the milk chocolate in a small heatproof bowl over (not touching) a saucepan of simmering water, stirring frequently, until just melted and smooth. Remove from the heat. Put the chocolate in a small sturdy plastic bag and snip off a corner. Squiggle the chocolate across the dates in a decorative fashion.

Cover and refrigerate to firm the filling and to set the chocolate. Serve chilled. Keep in the refrigerator, in a covered container, for up to 5 days.

Notes: Vienna almonds are almonds with a sugar coating; they are available in supermarkets or specialist nut or candy stores. You can use dried dates if fresh are not available.

Makes 15

praline liqueur-filled chocolate dates

fruit candies

200 g (7 oz) dried apricots	400 g (14 oz) sugar
200 g (7 oz) dried pears, roughly chopped	100 g (3½ oz/heaped 1 cup) flaked almonds, toasted

Put the apricots and pears in separate saucepans and generously cover with water. Bring to the boil over low–medium heat and simmer for about 40 minutes until tender. Check the water levels from time to time and add hot water if necessary to prevent the fruit from sticking to the pans.

When the fruit is tender, increase the heat and quickly boil off any excess water in the pans (otherwise the texture of the candies will be jammy rather than firm). Remove from the heat, add half the sugar to each and stir until the sugar melts. Set over low heat and bring to the boil. Simmer, stirring often, for 25–30 minutes, until the mixture comes away from the sides of the pan, but its texture is still a little chunky.

Line two 7 x 21 cm (2¾ x 8¼ inch) loaf tins with baking paper. Pour the apricots into one tin, the pears into the other. Leave overnight to firm up.

Put the almonds into a shallow bowl and break them up a little with your hands. Using a knife dipped in cold water, cut the fruit slabs into short rectangular bars and toss them in the almonds. The candies will keep in an airtight container for many weeks.

Makes about 60

rum truffles

200 g (7 oz/1¹/3 cups) finely
   chopped dark cooking
   chocolate
60 ml (2 fl oz/¹/4 cup) pouring
   (whipping) cream
30 g (1 oz) butter

50 g (1³/4 oz) chocolate cake,
   crumbled
2 teaspoons dark rum, brandy
   or whisky
95 g (3¹/4 oz/¹/2 cup) chocolate
   sprinkles

Line a baking tray with foil. Put the chocolate in a heatproof bowl. Combine the cream and butter in a small saucepan and stir over low heat until the butter melts and the mixture is just boiling. Pour the mixture over the chocolate and stir until the chocolate is melted and smooth.

Stir in the cake crumbs and rum. Refrigerate for 20 minutes, stirring occasionally, or until firm enough to handle. Roll heaped teaspoons of the mixture into balls.

Spread the chocolate sprinkles on a sheet of baking paper. Roll each truffle in the sprinkles until evenly coated, then place on the baking tray. Alternatively, the truffles can be rolled in unsweetened cocoa powder. Refrigerate for 30 minutes, or until firm.

Makes about 25

The Turkish name of this confection translates evocatively as 'rest for the throat' — what could be more enticing?

turkish delight

3 tablespoons powdered
   gelatine
450 g (1 lb/2 cups) sugar
1/2 teaspoon lemon juice
1 strip lemon zest, no pith
1/2 teaspoon tartaric acid
1–11/2 teaspoons rosewater,
   or to taste

pink food colouring or
   cochineal
100 g (31/2 oz/heaped 3/4 cup)
   icing sugar, sifted, combined
   with 3 tablespoons cornflour
   (cornstarch), to coat

Put 280 ml (91/2 fl oz) cold water in a heavy-based saucepan and sprinkle the gelatine in. Put over low heat and stir until the gelatine dissolves. Add the sugar, lemon juice and lemon zest and continue stirring until the sugar dissolves. Bring to the boil and boil for 8 minutes, stirring constantly. Discard the lemon zest.

Brush an 18 x 10 cm (7 x 4 inch) loaf (bar) tin with water.

Stir the tartaric acid and rosewater into the mixture. Add the food colouring, 2–3 drops at a time, until a very pale pink is reached. Pour into the prepared tin and leave overnight to set (do not put in the refrigerator).

Dust 3–4 tablespoons of the icing sugar mixture on a cold hard surface (marble is ideal) and put the rest into a shallow bowl. Ease the Turkish delight away from the sides of the tin with your fingers. Starting at one end, peel it out of the tin. It tends to be sticky and will stretch a little, but it is quite resilient. Place the slab on the icing-sugar-covered work surface.

Using an oiled knife, cut the Turkish delight into 2.5 cm (1 inch) squares and toss them in the bowl of icing sugar mixture to coat all sides. Work with a few at a time to prevent the uncoated pieces from sticking together. Store in an airtight container, with baking paper between each layer. It will keep for many weeks.

Makes 36

turkish delight

florentines

60 g (2¼ oz/¼ cup) butter, cubed

115 g (4 oz/½ cup) caster (superfine) sugar

125 ml (4 fl oz/½ cup) pouring (whipping) cream

125 g (4½ oz/1 cup) slivered almonds

70 g (2½ oz/⅓ cup) glacé (candied) cherries, finely chopped

55 g (2 oz/⅓ cup) mixed candied peel

55 g (2 oz/¼ cup) glacé (candied) ginger, finely chopped

40 g (1½ oz/⅓ cup) plain (all-purpose) flour

90 g (3¼ oz/scant ⅔ cup) chopped dark chocolate

90 g (3¼ oz/scant ⅔ cup) chopped white chocolate

Preheat the oven to 160°C (315°F/Gas 2–3). Line a large baking tray with baking paper. Put the butter, sugar and cream in a small saucepan and stir over low heat until smooth and combined. Bring just to the boil, then remove from the heat.

Combine the almonds, cherries, mixed peel, ginger and flour in a bowl. Stir in the butter mixture. Set aside for 5 minutes for the mixture to thicken a little.

Put small heaped teaspoonfuls, spaced well apart, onto the prepared tray. Flatten each to a 5 cm (2 inch) round. You will need to cook the biscuits in several batches. Bake for 12–15 minutes, or until a dark golden brown. Cool each batch on the tray, then transfer to a wire rack to cool completely and become crisp.

Put the dark and white chocolate in separate heatproof bowls and sit each bowl over (not touching) a saucepan of simmering water. Stir until the chocolate is just melted and smooth. Remove from the heat.

Using a metal spatula, coat the underside of half the biscuits with the dark chocolate and the remaining half with the white chocolate. Mark the chocolate with wavy lines using a fork, if desired. Put the biscuits on a wire rack, chocolate side up, to set.

Store in an airtight container for up to 5 days.

Makes 45

rocky road

250 g (9 oz/2¾ cups) pink and
white marshmallows, halved
160 g (5¾ oz/1 cup) unsalted
peanuts, roughly chopped
100 g (3½ oz/½ cup) glacé
(candied) cherries, halved

60 g (2¼ oz/1 cup) shredded
coconut
350 g (12 oz/2⅓ cups) chopped
dark chocolate

Line the base and two opposite sides of a shallow 20 cm (8 inch) square cake tin with foil.

Put the marshmallows, peanuts, cherries and coconut into a large bowl and mix until well combined.

Heat the chocolate in a heatproof bowl over (not touching) a bowl of simmering water, stirring occasionally, until just melted and smooth. Add the chocolate to the marshmallow mixture and toss until well combined. Spoon into the cake tin and press evenly over the base. Refrigerate for several hours, or until set. Carefully lift it out of the tin, then peel away the foil and cut the rocky road into small pieces. Store in an airtight container in the refrigerator.

Makes about 30 pieces

creamy coconut ice

250 g (9 oz/2 cups) icing
   (confectioners') sugar
1/4 teaspoon cream of tartar
395 g (14 oz) tin condensed milk

315 g (11 oz/3½ cups)
   desiccated (grated) coconut
2–3 drops pink food colouring
   or cochineal

Grease a 20 cm (8 inch) square cake tin and line the base and two opposite sides with baking paper, extending the paper over the sides for easy removal later.

Sift the icing sugar and cream of tartar into a bowl. Make a well in the centre and add the condensed milk. Using a wooden spoon, stir in half the coconut, then the remaining coconut. Mix well, using your hands. Divide the mixture in half and tint one half pink. Using your hands, knead the colour through evenly.

Press the pink mixture evenly over the base of the tin, then cover with the white mixture and press down firmly. Refrigerate for 1–2 hours, or until firm. Remove from the tin, remove the paper and cut into pieces. Store in an airtight container in a cool place for up to 3 weeks.

Makes 30 pieces

creamy coconut ice

These chocolate-coated confections are sure to be popular, so it's just as well the recipe makes a generous quantity.

chewy caramel and walnut logs

125 g (4^1/$_2$ oz/^{1}/$_2$ cup) butter, cubed

395 g (14 oz) can sweetened condensed milk

2 tablespoons golden syrup (light treacle)

160 g (5^3/$_4$ oz/^{3}/$_4$ cup firmly packed) light brown sugar

100 g (3^1/$_2$ oz/^{3}/$_4$ cup) walnuts, toasted, finely chopped

250 g (9 oz/1^2/$_3$ cups) chopped dark chocolate

Grease an 18 cm (7 inch) square slice tin and line it with baking paper, extending it over two opposite sides for easy removal later.

Stir the butter, condensed milk, golden syrup and brown sugar in a saucepan over low heat until the butter melts and the sugar dissolves. Increase the heat a little so that the mixture bubbles at a steady slow boil. Stir constantly for 9–10 minutes, or until caramel in colour and the mixture leaves the sides of the pan when stirred. Stir in the walnuts. Pour into the prepared tin and leave at room temperature to cool and set.

Remove from the tin, using the baking paper for handles. Cut into 6 even pieces. Gently roll each piece into a log approximately 12 cm (4^1/$_2$ inches) long and place on a tray lined with baking paper. Refrigerate for 1 hour, or until firm.

Melt the chocolate in a small bowl over a saucepan of simmering water, ensuring that the water doesn't touch the bottom of the bowl. Coat each caramel log with the chocolate, and put back onto the tray. Return to the refrigerator until set.

About 10 minutes before serving, take as many logs as you need at the time from the refrigerator. Cut into slices 1–1^1/$_2$ cm (about ^{1}/$_2$ inch) thick. Refrigerate the remainder in an airtight container for up to 1 week.

Makes about 70 pieces

sugared fruit cups

a selection of 20 pieces of small fruit, of a uniform size, with stalk attached (such as large green and purple grapes, cherries, cape gooseberries)

100 g (3¹/₂ oz) pure icing (confectioners') sugar, sifted
1 tablespoon Pear William or other fruit-based liqueur
about 1 teaspoon lemon juice
2 tablespoons caster (superfine) sugar

Snip grapes from the bunch, each with its stalk attached. Pull the dried leaves of cape gooseberries up and twist them together to form a fat stalk.

In a small bowl, stir together the icing sugar and liqueur. Add the lemon juice, a few drops at a time, until a thick, slowly flowing icing forms. Spread the caster sugar in a saucer. Working with 5–6 pieces of fruit at a time, hold each piece by the stalk and dip it in the icing to cover the bottom three-quarters. Gently shake off the excess. Sit it on a plate to dry a little. When you have 5–6 pieces, roll each in the sugar, starting with the first piece that you dipped. If the icing forms waves and doesn't allow an even coating of sugar, leave the fruit for little longer to dry slightly before sugaring. Sit the pieces on a clean plate while you coat the remainder. When the icing is dry, sit the fruits in mini foil or paper chocolate cups. They will keep, covered, in the refrigerator for up to 4 days.

Makes 20

dark chocolate nutty fudge

375 g (13 oz/2 cups) raw caster (superfine) sugar
170 ml (5 1/2 fl oz/2/3 cup) evaporated milk
20 g (3/4 oz) butter
100 g (3 1/2 oz) white marshmallows
250 g (9 oz/1 2/3 cups) chopped dark chocolate
125 g (4 1/2 oz) unsalted mixed nuts, toasted, roughly chopped
60 g (2 1/4 oz) white chocolate, chopped

Grease an 18 cm (7 inch) square slice tin and line it with baking paper. Heat the sugar, milk, and butter in a medium saucepan over low heat until the sugar dissolves. Increase the heat to medium, bring to the boil and simmer, stirring, for 4–5 minutes. Remove from the heat and stir in the marshmallows and dark chocolate. Continue stirring until smooth, adding the nuts at the end. Pour into the prepared tin and refrigerate until set.

Melt the white chocolate in a small bowl over (not touching) a saucepan of simmering water. Remove the chocolate nut mixture from the tin and cut into 16 squares. Put the squares on a sheet of baking paper, and using a piping bag, pipe the white chocolate in drizzly lines over the squares. Leave for the white chocolate to set before storing or eating. Store in an airtight container in the refrigerator. When ready to eat, bring out and leave at room temperature for 10 minutes to allow it to soften slightly.

Makes 16 pieces

dark chocolate nutty fudge

butterscotch meringue tart

shortcrust pastry
250 g (9 oz/2 cups) plain
    (all-purpose) flour
125 g (4¹/₂ oz/¹/₂ cup) chilled
    unsalted butter, chopped
2 tablespoons caster (superfine)
    sugar
1 egg yolk
1 tablespoon iced water

butterscotch filling
185 g (6¹/₂ oz/1 cup lightly
    packed) soft brown sugar

40 g (1¹/₂ oz/¹/₃ cup) plain
    (all-purpose) flour
250 ml (9 fl oz/1 cup) milk
45 g (1¹/₂ oz) unsalted butter
1 teaspoon natural vanilla
    extract
1 egg yolk

meringue
2 egg whites
2 tablespoons caster (superfine)
    sugar

Preheat the oven to 180°C (350°F/Gas 4). Grease a deep 22 cm (8¹/₂ inch) flan tin. Sift the flour into a large bowl and rub in the butter with your fingertips until the mixture resembles breadcrumbs. Stir in the sugar, egg yolk and water. Mix to a soft dough, then gather into a ball. Wrap in plastic wrap and chill for 20 minutes.

Roll the pastry between two sheets of baking paper until it is large enough to cover the base and sides of the tin. Transfer to the tin. Trim the edge and prick the pastry evenly with a fork. Chill again for 20 minutes. Line the pastry with a sheet of baking paper and spread baking beads or uncooked beans or rice over the paper. Bake for 35 minutes, then remove the paper and weights.

For the filling, place the sugar and flour in a small pan. Make a well in the centre and gradually whisk in the milk to form a smooth paste. Add the butter and whisk over low heat for 8 minutes, or until the mixture boils and thickens. Remove from the heat, add the vanilla and egg yolk and whisk until smooth. Spread into the pastry case and smooth the surface.

For the meringue, beat the egg whites until stiff peaks form. Add the sugar gradually, beating until thick and glossy and all the sugar has dissolved. Spoon over the filling and swirl into peaks with a fork or flat-bladed knife. Bake for 5–10 minutes, or until the meringue is golden. Serve warm or cold.

Serves 8–10

France's Normandy region is famed for its apples and cream, so any dish labelled 'normande' will feature these ingredients.

crepes normandes

crème normande
200 ml (7 fl oz) thickened (whipping) cream
1 teaspoon icing (confectioners') sugar, sifted
1–2 teaspoons Calvados (apple brandy)

crepes
75 g (2½ oz) plain (all-purpose) flour

1 egg
210 ml (7½ fl oz) milk
½ teaspoon natural vanilla extract
1 large granny smith apple
125 g (4½ oz/½ cup) unsalted butter
125 g (4½ oz/⅔ cup) raw caster (superfine) sugar

Combine the cream, icing sugar and Calvados in a small jug. Set aside while you make the crepes (the cream will thicken a little).

For the crepes, sift the flour and a small pinch of salt into a bowl. Combine the egg, milk and vanilla in a jug. Pour the liquid into the flour and whisk lightly until just combined.

Peel, core, quarter and very thinly slice the apples (use a mandoline if you have one). Melt a little butter in a crêpe pan over low–medium heat and add 5–6 apple slices. Fry without turning for about 2 minutes, or until they begin to darken.

Ladle a thin coating of batter over the top of the apples and cook for 50–60 seconds. Sprinkle with a tablespoon of sugar and cook for a further 50–60 seconds, until the sugar melts. Add more butter; when it has melted, flip the crepe over. Continue cooking until the crepe is crisp, about 45 seconds. Slide onto a plate and keep warm while cooking 5 more crepes in the same way, wiping the pan clean with a paper towel after each creepe.

Serve warm, drizzled with the cream mixture.

Serves 6

crêpes normandes

Ground hazelnuts give this meringue roll an interesting texture, and also serve to make it less sweet than the usual meringue.

hazelnut crackle log

70 g (2½ oz/½ cup) roasted
   skinned hazelnuts
4 egg whites, at room
   temperature
150 g (5½ oz/⅔ cup) caster
   (superfine) sugar
1 teaspoon cornflour
   (cornstarch)
1 teaspoon natural vanilla
   extract
1 teaspoon white wine vinegar

filling
2 teaspoons instant coffee
   granules
2 teaspoons hot water
225 g (8 oz/1 cup) mascarpone
   cheese
2 tablespoons sifted icing
   (confectioners') sugar

For the meringue, preheat the oven to 150°C (300°F/Gas 2). Draw a 20 x 35 cm (8 x 14 inch) rectangle on a sheet of baking paper. Put the sheet, pencil side down, on a baking tray.

Put the hazelnuts in a food processor and process until coarsely ground.

Whisk the egg whites in a large bowl until soft peaks form. Gradually add the sugar, 1 tablespoon at a time, and whisk until stiff and glossy. Gently fold in the hazelnuts, then the cornflour, vanilla and vinegar. Spoon onto the baking tray and spread evenly inside the marked rectangle. Bake for 25 minutes, or until the meringue is set and lightly golden.

Lay a large sheet of baking paper on a work surface and invert the cooked meringue on top. Peel off the baking paper that was used to line the baking tray and set the meringue aside to cool for 15 minutes.

To make the filling, dissolve the instant coffee in the hot water. Put the coffee, mascarpone and icing sugar in a bowl and mix well.

Using a palette knife, spread the filling evenly over the meringue. Starting at one short end and using the baking paper as a lever, gently roll up the meringue. The outer surface will crack into a pattern. Serve immediately, cut into slices.

Serves 8–10

chilled strawberry liqueur soufflé with strawberry compote

soufflé

250 g (9 oz/1²/₃ cups) strawberries, hulled

3 tablespoons strawberry or raspberry liqueur

1 tablespoon powdered gelatine

4 eggs, separated

125 g (4¹/₂ oz) caster (superfine) sugar

250 ml (9 fl oz/1 cup) thickened (whipping) cream

3 tablespoons caster (superfine) sugar, extra

strawberry compote

2 tablespoons icing (confectioners') sugar

2 tablespoons strawberry or raspberry liqueur, extra

250 g (9 oz/1²/₃ cups) strawberries, extra, hulled and chopped

Grease a 1.25-litre (44 fl oz/5 cup) soufflé dish and sprinkle with caster sugar. Tap out the excess. Put a collar on the dish (see Note).

Purée the strawberries and liqueur in a food processor. Set aside. Put the gelatine in a small bowl with 2 tablespoons cold water. Sit the bowl over a bowl of hot water to dissolve the gelatine.

In a medium bowl, whisk together the egg yolks and caster sugar. Set the bowl over a saucepan of simmering water and whisk until thick and pale,

2–3 minutes. Stir in the gelatine mixture and set aside until just cool, stirring occasionally.

Fold the strawberry purée into the gelatine mixture. Beat the cream until firm, then fold into the gelatine and strawberry mixture.

In a clean bowl, whisk the egg whites until soft peaks form. Whisking constantly, gradually add the extra caster sugar. Beat for 1–2 minutes until firm but not stiff. Gently fold the egg white mixture into the strawberry and cream mixture. Spoon into the prepared dish and smooth the surface. (The mixture will be above the rim of the dish.) Sit the dish on a flat tray. Refrigerate for at least 3 hours, or until firm.

For the compote, in a saucepan, stir together the sugar and liqueur over low heat until dissolved, then add the strawberries and toss through until warmed. To serve, carefully remove the paper collar from the soufflé. Spoon onto serving plates and serve with the compote.

Note: For the collar, cut a sheet of baking paper long enough to wrap around the dish. Fold it lengthways into thirds. Lightly grease the inside of the dish. Position the collar so that it protrudes about 7 cm (3 inches) above the dish and tie in position with jute or cotton (not plastic) string.

Serves 6–8

chilled strawberry liqueur soufflé with
strawberry compote

mini pastries with chocolate and vanilla cream

choux pastry
40 g (1¹/2 oz) butter, cubed
60 g (2¹/4 oz/¹/2 cup) plain
    (all-purpose) flour
2 eggs, lightly beaten
2 tablespoons flaked almonds

chocolate cream
125 ml (4 fl oz/¹/2 cup) milk
25 g (1 oz/¹/4 cup) chopped
    dark chocolate
1 egg yolk
1 tablespoon caster (superfine)
    sugar

vanilla cream
125 ml (4 fl oz/¹/2 cup) milk
¹/2 vanilla bean, split
1 egg yolk
1 tablespoon caster (superfine)
    sugar

200 ml (7 fl oz) thickened
    (whipping) cream
1 tablespoon icing
    (confectioners') sugar, plus
    extra, to dust

Preheat the oven to 220°C (425°F/Gas 7). On a large sheet of baking paper, mark out four 9 cm (3¹/2 inch) rounds. Lightly grease a baking tray and line with the baking paper, pencil side down.

For the pastry, put the butter and 125 ml (4 fl oz/¹/2 cup) water in a saucepan and gently heat until the butter melts. Bring to the boil over medium heat, then remove from the heat and add the flour, mixing well with a wooden spoon to combine. Return to the heat and cook, stirring, until the mixture leaves the sides of the pan and forms a ball.

Transfer the mixture to a bowl and gradually beat in the eggs using electric beaters. Continue beating until smooth and glossy. Transfer to a large piping bag with a plain piping nozzle. Pipe circular mounds of mixture inside the drawn lines on the paper. Sprinkle the tops with almonds. Bake for 10 minutes, then reduce the temperature to 180°C (350°F/Gas 4) and bake for about 15 minutes more, or until puffed and golden. Cut in half using a serrated knife and bake for 3–5 minutes more, until the centres are dry. Cool on a wire rack while you make the cream mixtures.

For the chocolate cream, heat the milk and chocolate in a small saucepan over low heat, stirring, until the chocolate melts. Bring almost to boiling point, then remove from the heat. Mix the egg yolk and sugar in a small bowl, then gradually add the hot milk, whisking continually. Pour the mixture back into the saucepan and stir over low heat until thickened. Pour into a serving jug and allow to cool.

For the vanilla cream, put the milk in a small saucepan. Scrape the seeds from the vanilla bean into the milk, then add the pod also. Bring almost to boiling point, then remove from the heat. Mix the egg yolk and sugar in a small bowl, then gradually add the hot milk, whisking continually. Pour the mixture back into the saucepan and stir over low heat until thickened. Strain into a serving jug and allow to cool.

When ready to serve, whip the cream until firm peaks form, gradually adding the icing sugar towards the end. Fill the pastries with this mixture. Sit a pastry on each of four serving plates, dust with icing sugar and serve at once, with the jugs of sauce on the side.

Makes 4

hazelnut and coffee meringue torte

meringue
375 g (13 oz/2^2/3 cups)
hazelnuts, roasted and
skinned (see Note, page 41)
8 egg whites
200 g (7 oz) caster (superfine)
sugar
40 g (1^1/2 oz/^{1}/3 cup) plain
(all-purpose) flour

150 g (5^1/2 oz/1 cup) chopped
dark chocolate

filling
4 tablespoons icing
(confectioners') sugar
1^1/2 tablespoons instant coffee
granules
600 ml (21 fl oz) thickened
(whipping) cream

384

Preheat the oven to 150°C (300°F/Gas 2). Draw a 22 cm (8^1/2 inch) circle on three sheets of baking paper. Lay one sheet, pencil side down, on each of three baking trays.

In a food processor, pulse the hazelnuts until chopped to a medium-coarse texture. Reserve ^{1}/4 cup for later.

In a large bowl, whisk the egg whites until stiff peaks form. Gradually add the sugar, whisking constantly until thick and glossy. Gently fold in the flour and nuts.

Divide the mixture among the trays, spreading it out evenly to fill the circles. Bake for 25–30 minutes until light golden brown. They will be cake-like, not like a typical crisp meringue. If you need to use three oven racks, the trays will need to be swapped around during cooking for even browning. Cool on the trays, then invert and peel off the baking paper.

Meanwhile, melt the chocolate in a small bowl set over a saucepan of simmering water, ensuring that the water doesn't touch the bottom of the bowl. Spread one-third of the chocolate over each of two meringue rounds. Refrigerate the meringue rounds while the filling is being made.

In a bowl, dissolve the icing sugar and coffee in $1^1/_2$ tablespoons warm water. Add the cream and whip until thick.

Put one chocolate-coated meringue layer onto a serving plate, chocolate side up. Spread with one-third of the filling, leaving the edges uncovered as the filling will ooze out as the layers are added. Repeat the layering. Put the plain meringue on top and spread with the last one-third of filling. Sprinkle with the reserved hazelnuts. Spoon the remaining melted chocolate into a small piping bag (or a sturdy plastic bag with one corner snipped off) and drizzle decorative stripes across the cream and nuts.

Serves 8

hazelnut and coffee meringue torte

almond, orange and quince tarts

pastry
175 g (6 oz) plain (all-purpose)
  flour
50 g (1³/4 oz/heaped ¹/3 cup)
  icing (confectioners') sugar
100 g (3¹/2 oz) unsalted butter,
  cubed
1 egg yolk
3–4 drops natural vanilla
  extract

filling
85 g (3 oz/¹/2 cup) raw caster
  (superfine) sugar
85 g (3 oz/¹/3 cup) unsalted
  butter, softened
2 eggs
2 teaspoons finely grated
  orange zest
50 g (1³/4 oz/¹/2 cup) ground
  almonds
125 g (4¹/2 oz/1 cup) toasted
  slivered almonds
100 g (3¹/2 oz) quince paste,
  thinly sliced

whipped cream or vanilla bean
  ice cream, to serve

For the pastry, process the flour, icing sugar, butter, egg yolk and vanilla in a food processor until just smooth. Form into a ball, cover with plastic wrap and chill for 45 minutes.

Grease six 8 cm (3^{1}/4 inch) loose-based tart tins. Roll the pastry out thinly on a lightly floured surface and it use to line the prepared tins. Chill the pastry-lined tins while the oven preheats.

Preheat the oven to 180°C (350°F/Gas 4). Line the pastry tins with baking paper, cover the base of each with pastry weights or uncooked beans or rice and bake for 10 minutes. Remove the baking paper and weights and return to the oven for 5 minutes. Cool while making the filling.

For the filling, beat the sugar and butter together until smooth, then add the eggs one at a time, beating well after each addition. Don't worry if the mixture separates. Stir through the orange zest and the ground and slivered almonds.

Place the quince paste slices in the bottom of each tart shell, dividing them evenly among the tart shells. Divide the filling among the pastry cases and bake for about 20 minutes, or until set.

Serve warm, with whipped cream or vanilla bean ice cream.

Makes 6

caramel tarts with chocolate ganache

ganache
100 g (3^1/$_2$ oz/^{2}/$_3$ cup) chopped
    dark chocolate
2 tablespoons pouring
    (whipping) cream

pastry
150 g (5^1/$_2$ oz/1^1/$_4$ cups) plain
    (all-purpose) flour
90 g (3^1/$_4$ oz/^{1}/$_3$ cup) chilled
    unsalted butter, cubed
65 g (2^1/$_2$ oz/heaped ^{1}/$_4$ cup)
    caster (superfine) sugar

filling
395 g (13^3/$_4$ oz) can sweetened
    condensed milk
30 g (1 oz) unsalted butter
2 tablespoons golden syrup
    (light treacle)

1^1/$_2$ tablespoons pistachio nuts,
    to garnish (see Note)

For the ganache, melt the chocolate and cream in a bowl over a saucepan of simmering water, stirring well to combine. Remove from the heat, cool, then refrigerate for 10–15 minutes until firm but not solid.

Preheat the oven to 180°C (350°F/Gas 4). Grease a 12-hole patty tin (each hole 40 ml/1^1/$_4$ fl oz capacity). Run a strip of foil across the base and up two sides of each hole, leaving a bit of overhang. These will act as handles to aid removal of the tarts later on.

For the pastry, put the flour, butter and sugar into a food processor and pulse until the mixture resembles breadcrumbs. Divide among the prepared patty tin holes and firmly press the mixture down onto the bases with your fingers. Bake for 12–15 minutes until lightly golden in colour. While they are still hot, press the bases down with the back of a small teaspoon, as they will have risen a little.

For the filling, put the condensed milk, butter and golden syrup in a small saucepan over low heat. Stir until the butter has melted. Increase the heat to medium and simmer for 2–3 minutes, stirring constantly, until light caramel in colour. When stirring, ensure that the bottom and sides of the pan are scraped to prevent the mixture from catching and scorching.

Divide the caramel among the pastry bases and cool for 5 minutes. Gently remove the tarts from the tin; transfer to a wire rack to cool completely.

To serve, whisk the ganache well. Put into a piping bag with a medium-sized star nozzle and pipe swirls of ganache on top of the caramel. Sprinkle with the pistachios. Store in the refrigerator, covered; remove from the refrigerator 10–15 minutes before eating.

Note: The pistachios can be toasted in the oven after the tart bases bake.

Makes 12

caramel tarts with
chocolate ganache

creamy ginger and nut log

filling
100 g (3^1/$_2$ oz) caster (superfine) sugar
100 g (3^1/$_2$ oz) butter, softened
500 g (1 lb 2 oz/2 cups) farm cheese or Neufchatel
^{1}/$_2$ teaspoon grated orange zest
^{1}/$_2$ teaspoon grated lemon zest
1 teaspoon natural vanilla extract
1 egg
25 g (1 oz/^{1}/$_4$ cup) pecans
25 g (1 oz) glacé (candied) ginger

biscuit (cookie) layers
about 24 small (8 cm/3^1/$_4$ inch long) savoiardi (sponge finger) biscuits
about 125 ml (4 fl oz/^{1}/$_2$ cup) green ginger wine

chocolate glaze
150 g (5^1/$_2$ oz/1 cup) chopped dark chocolate
2 tablespoons green ginger wine
50 g (1^3/$_4$ oz/^{1}/$_4$ cup) caster (superfine) sugar
40 g (1^1/$_2$ oz) butter, cubed

For the filling, process the sugar and butter in a food processor until pale. Add the cheese and process until smooth. Transfer to a bowl, add the citrus zests, vanilla and egg and mix well. Chop the pecans and ginger to a medium-fine texture and fold through the cheese mixture.

To assemble, run a double thickness of foil across the base of a 8 x 16 x 9 cm (3^1/$_4$ x 6^1/$_4$ x 3^1/$_2$ inch) loaf tin, allowing for plenty of overhang to remove the loaf later on. Line the base with a single layer of savoiardi, flat side down (the length of the biscuits should run the length of the tin). If necessary, trim the biscuits to fit snugly. Sprinkle liberally with green ginger wine, but not so much that the biscuits become soggy. Line both sides of the tin with a single layer of biscuits in a similar manner, flat side out and running in the same direction as those on the base. Sprinkle with more green ginger wine. Spread one half of the filling over them, packing it in firmly, and cover this with another layer of biscuits. Sprinkle with more green ginger wine. Spread the remaining filling on top and cover with the last of the biscuits, this time with the flat side uppermost. The filling and biscuits should end up on the same level; trim the biscuits if necessary. Sprinkle with the last of the wine. Wrap the tin in foil and leave in the refrigerator overnight to set.

For the chocolate glaze, melt the chocolate with the ginger wine in a bowl set over a pan of simering water, stirring occasionally until smooth. Remove from the heat and stir in the sugar, then the butter; stir until smooth and glossy. If necessary, beat in a little water, a teaspoon at a time, to give a spoonable consistency.

Turn the loaf out onto a wire cake rack set over a tray. Remove the foil then spoon the glaze all over, completely covering the top and sides. Leave until set (the glaze will remain slightly soft). Cut into slices to serve.

Serves 8

blueberry and lavender pancake stack

raspberry sauce
150 g (5^1/2 oz/1^1/4 cups) fresh
  raspberries
1 tablespoon clear honey
1 teaspoon lemon juice

maple cream
375 ml (13 fl oz/1^1/2 cups) crème
  fraîche
2–3 tablespoons pure maple
  syrup

pancakes
1 teaspoon grated lemon zest
2 tablespoons pouring
  (whipping) cream

1 egg, separated
175 ml (5^1/2 fl oz/^{2}/3 cup) milk
50 g (1^3/4 oz/heaped ^{1}/3 cup)
  plain (all-purpose) flour
2 teaspoons caster (superfine)
  sugar
1 teaspoon unsprayed lavender
  flowers (stripped off the
  stalk)
150 g (5^1/2 oz/1 cup) fresh
  blueberries

unsalted butter, for frying
a few unsprayed lavender
  flowers, extra, to garnish

For the raspberry sauce, process the raspberries, honey and lemon juice in a food processor until smooth. Pass through a fine sieve; discard the seeds.

For the maple cream, beat the crème fraîche and maple syrup together until smooth.

For the pancakes, mix together the lemon zest, cream, egg yolk and milk in a jug. Sift the flour into a bowl. Stir in the sugar and lavender flowers and pour in the liquid. Whisk to a smooth batter.

In a clean bowl, whisk the egg white until stiff. Using a metal spoon, gently fold the egg white into the batter.

Melt a small knob of butter in a crepe pan or non-stick frying pan. Spoon in enough batter, roughly 1^1/$_2$ tablespoons, to make an 8 cm (3^1/$_4$ inch) pancake and scatter some blueberries on top. When small bubbles begin to break on the surface, flip the pancake over. Fry for another minute or two, until golden on both sides and cooked through. Transfer to a warm plate and keep covered. Once you get the hang of it you can make 3 or 4 pancakes at once. Repeat, using up all the batter, and wiping the pan clean with a paper towel between each batch of pancakes. You will need 12 pancakes; there is enough batter to allow for a couple of failures.

Put a pancake on each of four serving plates and top with a heaped tablespoon of maple cream. Repeat twice more, finishing with a final dollop of cream. Drizzle the raspberry sauce around the edges and scatter the extra lavender flowers over the lot. Serve at once.

Serves 4

blueberry and lavender pancake stack

date and pecan puddings with brandied toffee sauce

35 g (1^1/4 oz/^{1}/3 cup) pecans, chopped
180 g (6^1/2 oz/1 cup) pitted dates, chopped
1 teaspoon natural vanilla extract
^{3}/4 teaspoon bicarbonate of soda (baking soda)
90 g (3^1/4 oz/^{1}/3 cup) butter, softened
140 g (5 oz/^{2}/3 cup) caster (superfine) sugar
2 eggs
185 g (6^1/2 oz/1^1/2 cups) self-raising flour, sifted

brandied toffee sauce
185 g (6^1/2 oz/1 cup lightly packed) soft brown sugar
250 ml (9 fl oz/1 cup) pouring (whipping) cream
60 g (2^1/4 oz/^{1}/4 cup) butter, cubed
1 teaspoon natural vanilla extract
2–3 tablespoons brandy, to taste

pouring (whipping) cream, to serve (optional)

Preheat the oven to 180ºC (350ºF/Gas 4). Grease six 250 ml (9 fl oz/1 cup) metal or ceramic moulds and scatter the chopped pecans over the base. Put the moulds on a baking tray.

In a heatproof bowl, combine the dates and boiling water. Stir in the vanilla and bicarbonate of soda. Set aside to cool and to soften the dates.

In a bowl, beat the butter and sugar with electric beaters for 2 minutes until thick and creamy. Add the eggs one at a time, beating well between each addition. Fold in the sifted flour with a metal spoon, then fold in the date mixture. Spoon the mixture into the prepared moulds, filling them three-quarters full. Bake for about 25 minutes, or until firm to the touch and well risen.

For the toffee sauce, combine the sugar, cream, butter and vanilla in a small saucepan. Stir over low heat to dissolve the sugar, then bring to the boil. Simmer for 10–15 minutes until slightly thickened. Remove from the heat, cool a little, then stir in the brandy to taste.

Remove the puddings from the oven, set aside for 5 minutes, then with the aid of a small, flat-bladed knife, turn them out onto serving plates. Pour the hot sauce over and serve with some cream, if liked.

Notes: The puddings should be served hot, with the sauce a little absorbed into them. If not serving immediately after cooking, you can microwave the puddings and reheat the sauce. The puddings can be frozen for up to a month; before serving, thaw them, then microwave to reheat them. The sauce will keep, refrigerated, for a week.

Serves 6

sticky almond caramel puddings with almond toffee shards and amaretto cream

almond toffee
175 g (6 oz/3/4 cup) caster (superfine) sugar
50 g (13/4 oz/1/3 cup) unblanched whole almonds, toasted

puddings
100 g (31/2 oz) unsalted butter, softened
125 g (41/2 oz/2/3 cup lightly packed) dark brown sugar
2 eggs
175 g (6 oz/11/3 cups) self-raising flour
3 tablespoons buttermilk

1 teaspoon natural vanilla extract
50 g (13/4 oz/1/3 cup) unblanched whole almonds, chopped

caramel sauce
85 g (3 oz/1/3 cup firmly packed) dark brown sugar
20 g (3/4 oz) unsalted butter
150 ml (5 fl oz) thickened (whipping) cream

amaretto cream
80 ml (21/2 fl oz/1/3 cup) thickened (whipping) cream
1 teaspoon Amaretto (almond liqueur)

For the almond toffee, slowly heat the sugar and 2 tablespoons water in a saucepan, stirring and brushing down the sides of the pan with water, until the sugar melts. Increase the heat to medium and simmer without stirring for 3 minutes, or until it is a light golden colour. Put a sheet of foil on a baking tray and scatter the almonds in a single layer in the middle.

Remove the toffee from the heat, let the bubbles subside, then pour it over the nuts. Quickly tilt the tray to get an even coating. Leave to harden.

For the puddings, grease six tall 185 ml (6 fl oz/¾ cup) dariole moulds. Line the bases with a circle of baking paper. Using electric beaters, beat the butter and sugar in a bowl until light and fluffy. Beat in the eggs one at a time. Gradually fold in the flour, then stir in the buttermilk and vanilla. Fold in the almonds. Divide among the prepared moulds, filling them just over halfway. Level the tops. Cover each with a circle of baking paper. Cut six squares of foil about 5 cm (2 inches) larger than the top of the moulds and fold each square loosely over a mould, leaving a space underneath for the puddings to expand. Tie the foil onto the moulds. Place a round wire rack (or a scrunched-up large piece of foil) in the bottom of a saucepan just large enough (about 25 cm/10 inches in diameter) to take the moulds standing up. Carefully pour cold water into the saucepan to come about 4 cm (1½ inches) up the sides of the moulds. Cover the pan and bring to the boil over medium heat. Lower the heat and simmer for 30 minutes.

For the caramel sauce, stir the sugar and butter in a small saucepan over low heat until the butter melts. Add the cream and simmer for 5 minutes. For the Amaretti cream, mix the cream and Amaretti together well. To serve, unmould the puddings onto serving plates, spoon over the caramel sauce and drizzle the Amaretto cream around the base. Break the toffee into shards and put a couple in the top of each pudding. Serve at once.

Serves 6

sticky almond caramel puddings with
almond toffee shards and amaretto cream

hazelnut coffee cream cake

hazelnut topping
30 g (1 oz) butter, melted
2 tablespoons caster (superfine)
  sugar
2 tablespoons golden syrup
  (light treacle)
140 g (5 oz/1 cup) hazelnuts,
  roasted and skinned (see
  Note, page 41)

cake
3 eggs, separated
125 g (4$^1/_2$ oz) caster (superfine)
  sugar
1 teaspoon natural vanilla
  extract
85 g (3 oz/$^2/_3$ cup) cornflour
  (cornstarch)

1 teaspoon baking powder
100 g (3$^1/_2$ oz/scant 1 cup)
  roasted, skinned and ground
  hazelnuts (see Note, page 41)

coffee cream
170 ml (5$^1/_2$ fl oz/$^2/_3$ cup)
  thickened (whipping) cream
3 teaspoons icing
  (confectioners') sugar
1 teaspoon instant coffee
  granules
1 tablespoon Tia Maria or other
  coffee liqueur

icing (confectioners') sugar,
  to dust

Preheat the oven to 180°C (350°F/Gas 4). Grease a 23 cm (9 inch) round cake tin and line the base with baking paper.

For the hazelnut topping, combine the melted butter, caster sugar and golden syrup in a small bowl. Roughly chop half of the hazelnuts. Scatter the whole and chopped hazelnuts over the base of the prepared tin. Drizzle the butter mixture carefully over the nuts and spread evenly.

In a small bowl, beat the egg whites to firm peaks with electric beaters, gradually adding the sugar. Beat for 3 minutes, or until thick and glossy. Beat in the egg yolks one at a time, then the vanilla extract. Transfer the mixture to a larger bowl. Using a metal spoon, fold in the combined sifted cornflour and baking powder alternately with the ground hazelnuts.

Carefully spoon the mixture into the prepared tin over the hazelnuts. Smooth the surface. Bake for about 35 minutes until well risen, firm and brown, and a skewer inserted into the centre of the cake comes out clean. Leave in the tin for 10 minutes before turning onto a wire rack to cool completely. If any nuts have stuck to the baking paper, return them to the top of the cake.

For the coffee cream, beat the cream and icing sugar until thick. Dissolve the coffee granules in 1 teaspoon warm water. Beat the coffee and liqueur into the cream. To assemble, cut the cake in half horizontally. Spread the bottom half thickly with the cream and place the other half on top, with the hazelnuts facing up. Dust the hazelnuts with icing sugar.

Serves 8–10

baked rhubarb amaretto cream millefeuilles

amaretto cream
2 egg yolks
2 tablespoons caster (superfine)
    sugar
1 tablespoon plain (all-purpose)
    flour
185 ml (6 fl oz/¾ cup) milk
2 tablespoons Amaretto
    (almond liqueur)

350 g (12 oz) rhubarb, leaves
    removed, stems washed,
    trimmed and cut into 5 cm
    (2 inch) lengths (you will
    need about 225 g/
    8 oz after trimming)

3 tablespoons caster (superfine)
    sugar
3 tablespoons white wine or
    verjuice

2 sheets frozen butter puff pastry
1 egg

3 tablespoons thickened
    (whipping) cream
icing (confectioners') sugar,
    to dust

For the amaretto cream, beat the egg yolks, sugar and flour until creamy in a small bowl using electric beaters. Put the milk in a small saucepan and bring slowly to the boil. Slowly pour into the egg and milk mixture with the beaters running. Return the mixture to the saucepan and whisk constantly until the mixture boils and thickens. Remove from the heat and stir in the liqueur. Pour into a bowl, cover and refrigerate until cold.

Preheat the oven to 180°C (350°F/Gas 4). Put the rhubarb pieces into a baking dish that holds them in one layer. Sprinkle the sugar and wine or verjuice over, then bake for 20 minutes, or until tender but still retaining shape. Cool in the juices, then chill.

Increase the heat to 220°C (425°F/Gas 7). Line a large baking tray with baking paper. Brush the pastry sheets with egg beaten with 2 teaspoons water. Cut each pastry sheet into 9 even squares. Arrange on the prepared tray, well spaced. You may need to do this in two batches. Prick the pastry squares all over with a fork. Bake for 10–12 minutes until golden brown and puffed. Remove from the oven and trim away any edges that are stuck together, so that the pastry flakes are visible. Allow to cool.

Assemble the millefeuilles just prior to serving. Beat the cream to soft peaks and gently fold into the amaretto cream. Put each of 6 squares of pastry onto serving plates and put a spoonful of custard onto the centre of each. Cover with some of the rhubarb and a drizzle of juice. Put another square of pastry on top (there is no need to be too formal; the stacks can be slightly angled and freeform) and press down gently. Add another spoonful of cream and the remaining rhubarb and juice. Top with the final layer of pastry and dust liberally with icing sugar.

Serves 6

index

411

413

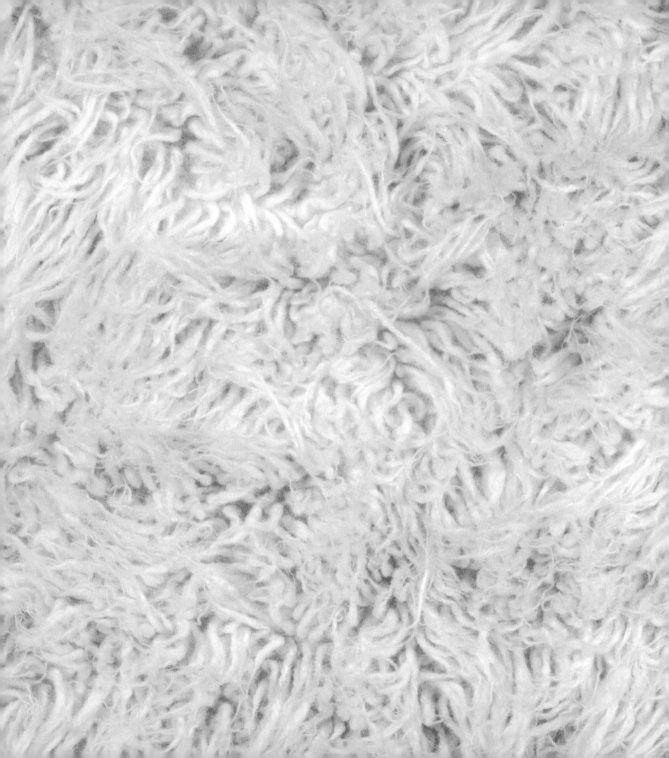